ENGLISH BINDING BEFORE 1500

ENGLISH BINDING
BEFORE 1500

BY

G. D. HOBSON, M.A. Oxon.

Author of
Bindings in Cambridge Libraries
etc.

THE SANDARS LECTURES
1927

CAMBRIDGE
AT THE UNIVERSITY PRESS
1929

CAMBRIDGE UNIVERSITY PRESS
Cambridge, New York, Melbourne, Madrid, Cape Town, Singapore,
São Paulo, Delhi, Dubai, Tokyo, Mexico City

Cambridge University Press
The Edinburgh Building, Cambridge CB2 8RU, UK

Published in the United States of America by Cambridge University Press, New York

www.cambridge.org
Information on this title: www.cambridge.org/9780521137287

First published 1929
First paperback printing 2010

A catalogue record for this publication is available from the British Library

ISBN 978-0-521-13728-7 Paperback

TO

STRICKLAND GIBSON

CONTENTS

APPENDICES

PLATES

At end

PLATES

ACKNOWLEDGEMENTS

I HAVE to thank the Syndics of the University Press for permission to reprint Plates 26 and 27, and the greater part of Appendices B and E, from *Bindings in Cambridge Libraries*: their kindness has enabled me to concentrate in this volume all that I have to say at present on the earliest bindings decorated with metal stamps. To Dr M. J. Husung I am indebted for leave to reproduce the cut on the title from the Prussian State Library's copy of Erhart Grosse, *Hye heben sich an drei bücher des doctrinals* (Hain 8084; Voullième 2697). To all owners and custodians of the bindings illustrated I offer my sincere thanks for permitting their publication, and I have to thank also the Director of the Victoria and Albert Museum, South Kensington, for leave to reproduce Weale's two rubbings (Pls. 24 and 25)—the only discoverable record of what I fear is a destroyed binding. Many librarians have given me valuable help, particularly Miss Bull, of Hereford Cathedral Library; Monsieur Morel-Payen, of the Bibliothèque de la Ville, Troyes; Mr Strickland Gibson, of Bodley's Library; Dr H. Thomas and Mr Eric Millar of the British Museum; Canon Kynaston, of Lincoln Cathedral Library; Professor Minns, of Pembroke College; Canon Blake, of Worcester Cathedral Library; and Mr J. B. Oldham, of Shrewsbury School. Mr H. R. Creswick has read the proofs with his usual care, and Mr E. P. Goldschmidt told me of the six Romanesque bindings in the library at Admont.

G. D. H.

1929

ABBREVIATIONS

Birkenmajer.—Aleksander Birkenmajer. *Oprawa Rekopisu* 2470 *Bibljoteki Jagiellonskiej*. Krakow, 1925.

Brassington, *History*.—W. S. Brassington, F.S.A. *A History of the Art of Bookbinding*. 1894.

Burlington.—Burlington Fine Arts Club, *Exhibition of Bookbindings*. 1891.

Fletcher, *Bindings*.—W. Y. Fletcher, F.S.A. *English Bookbindings*. 1896.

Fletcher, *English*.—W. Y. Fletcher. *English Bookbindings in the British Museum*. 1895.

Gaselee.—Stephen Gaselee, M.A., F.S.A., C.B.E. *The Early Printed Books in the Library of Corpus Christi College, Cambridge*. A Handlist. Cambridge, 1921.

Gibson, *Bodley*.—Strickland Gibson. *Some notable Bodleian Bindings*. Oxford, 1901–4.

Gottlieb.—Dr T. Gottlieb. *K. K. Hofbibliothek Bucheinbände*. Vienna, 1910.

Haseloff.—*Miscellanea Francesco Ehrle*. Vol. v. Rome, 1924. Pp. 507–528. Arthur Haseloff, *Der Einband der HS. des Marcusevangeliums des Harderadus*.

Jahrbuch, II.—*Jahrbuch der Einbandkunst, Erster* (*Zweiter*) *Jahrgang*. 1927–9.

Podlaha.—*Topographie der historischen und Kunst-Denkmale im Königreiche Böhmen*. Vol. I, Pt. II. *Die Bibliothek des Metropolitan-Kapitels verfasst von Dr Anton Podlaha*. Prague, 1904.

Thirty Bindings.—*Thirty Bindings, described by G. D. Hobson, selected from the First Edition Club's seventh exhibition* 1926.

I

The Early Bindings: before 1300

I DO NOT PROPOSE TO DEAL IN THESE LECTURES WITH embroidered or metal bindings; apart from other considerations, the material for such a study is lacking since only one English medieval embroidered[1] binding exists, and only one early metal[2] binding which may be of English workmanship. The earliest decorated leather[3] binding is also unique (Pl. 1); and to this loneliness it owes much of its mystery and peculiar fascination. It is of red goatskin over thin boards of lime-wood, and as will be seen is decorated entirely with the knife or graver, no figured stamps being used; some of the lines are painted in yellow or silver. The binding covers a manuscript of St John's Gospel, belonging to Stonyhurst College, which is celebrated on account of the inscription, in a 13th-century hand, that it was taken from the coffin of St Cuthbert in 1104. There can be no doubt of the trustworthiness of the inscription, for it is copied from another, now very faint and hardly legible, which is in an early 12th-century hand. The only possible argument against it is the statement in a contemporary inventory that the book found on the inner coffin of St Cuthbert in 1104 was a copy of the Gospels, not St John's Gospel only; but we need not attach much weight to the discrepancy, since no inventory that was ever compiled is free from mistakes.

St Cuthbert died in 687; and his coffin was opened no less than four times—in 699, 740, 875 and 1104. The binding, therefore, must either be earlier than 875 or later than 1104, and there can be no hesitation in deciding for the earlier date on grounds of style alone, for no single feature of the binding recalls 12th-century work. More difficult is the question whether this is the original binding or a work of the 8th or 9th century, since no other specimen of early Northumbrian leatherwork is known with which it may be compared. Indeed, decorated leatherwork of any kind or any country earlier than A.D. 1000 is exceedingly scarce; there are a few Coptic bindings[4] in foreign libraries; a few Irish satchels[5] for books or shrines; and three 9th-century[5] bindings in the Library at Fulda; but apart from these, so far as I know, there is nothing. None of these is very like the Stonyhurst binding; and yet they are more like it than is any later work. Parallels to some features of the binding may be found on other early Northumbrian works of art; the bosses on the upper cover recall the Ormside bowl[6], which is certainly earlier than A.D. 900; interlacings such as those above and below may be found on St Cuthbert's portable altar[7] and on many early manuscripts, both

[1] On the Felbrigge Psalter, a 13th-century manuscript in the British Museum; reproduced and described by Mr Cyril Davenport in *English Embroidered Bookbindings*, 1899, Pl. 3 and p. 29, and by Prof. W. R. Lethaby in the *Burlington Magazine* for October, 1928.

[2] Or rather a binding with metal ornaments other than the usual cornerpieces or bosses; this is a little book with a bronze figure of Christ crucified, and is said by a very improbable tradition to be the volume on which our medieval kings and queens took their coronation oaths; reproduced and described by Mr Davenport in *Royal English Bookbindings*, 1896, Pl. I and p. 8.

[3] I am greatly indebted to Mr G. H. Palmer, of the Art Library, Victoria and Albert Museum, South Kensington, for permission to use the notes which he made on this binding when it was on loan there a few years ago. It was examined then by various English experts on Anglo-Saxon art, who agreed that it was not later than the 9th or 10th century; my own opinion of its early date was formed before I knew this.

[4] See Loubier, *Der Bucheinband*, Leipzig, 1926, pp. 118–121 and his references.

[5] See Appendix A for a note on these early satchels and bindings, and a possible design for another binding of the period.

[6] Described and illustrated by Professor Baldwin Brown, *The Arts in Early England*, Vol. V, 1921, Pls. XXX and XXXI.

[7] Baldwin Brown, op. cit. Pl. XLII.

Irish and Anglo-Saxon; but such comparisons are unconvincing, since a type of ornament may be used by one set of craftsmen for many years before it is adopted by another.

We are thrown back then on other considerations; and if all the circumstances are taken into account, there would seem to be good grounds for believing this to be a work of the 7th century and the original binding of the book. For in 875 the manuscript had not been in existence much more than 200 years, and during practically the whole of that time it had lain undisturbed in St Cuthbert's coffin. But a good morocco binding ought not to need renewal after a placid existence of only two centuries; many fine early 18th-century bindings survive, which are almost as fresh now as the day they were executed, and these too no fugitive and cloistered volumes such as the book we are examining, but active citizens of the world of books. For most of the eight centuries and a quarter that have passed since the book was taken from the coffin, it has been guarded with pious care; and this vigilance amply accounts for its wonderful preservation, which has misled some students into doubting its antiquity. It is probable, therefore, that in this binding we have a product of 7th-century Northumbrian art, and the original cover placed on the book in St Cuthbert's lifetime[1].

Very different from the Stonyhurst book are the next bindings to be considered—a family of 12th- and early 13th-century bindings, which I propose to call Romanesque. Instead of being dull red, the leather of which they are made is usually dark brown[2]; instead of having a pattern drawn with a knife or graver, they are decorated with repeated impressions of figured metal stamps; and instead, finally, of surviving in one lonely specimen, no less than forty-seven[3] of these Romanesque bindings are known. Attention was first called to them by the late W. H. J. Weale, who described or mentioned twenty-two of them; eighteen of these are in English libraries, seven out of the eighteen at Durham; and Weale described them generally as being of English, and chiefly Durham, workmanship. True, he admitted that some might be 'Anglo-Norman'; but he left his readers with the impression that the art was an English invention; that the finest of these bindings were English; and that even the foreign specimens were executed under English influence.

This view is no longer tenable; in recent years twenty-five more Romanesque bindings have come to light; all but three of these are in continental libraries; so that of the forty-seven now known, we possess twenty-one only. Of the other twenty-six, eight are in France, fourteen in German-speaking towns within the limits of the Holy Roman Empire, one in Bohemia, two in Poland, and one in Spain. The old English preponderance of ownership has gone; and with it have gone the assumptions to which it gave rise.

The comprehensive survey made possible by the new discoveries proves that the art of decorating bindings with figured stamps was not English, but international[4]; it was in fact one manifestation of that 12th-century Renaissance to which we owe, among much else, the revival of monumental sculpture. It is not, therefore, surprising to find

[1] It is, of course, not certain that the book was ever bound in St Cuthbert's lifetime (cf. Appendix K); but the binding seems a practical cover for a book in daily use, and it is probable that the little volume would have been more gloriously arrayed if it had not been bound till it had already become the precious relic of a great saint.

[2] No. XXI is an exception, being of white doe-skin stained pink.

[3] See Appendix B.

[4] Perhaps this is too strong a term; all the finest of the surviving bindings are either French or English.

in little on these bindings what is shown more amply on the façades and porches of 12th-century churches—on both we find Biblical subjects such as Samson[1] and the lion, the tree of Jesse, David with his harp, the Virgin and Child, the Agnus Dei, the Holy Dove, St Peter, St Paul and the four and twenty Elders described in the Apocalypse, who with crowns and harps and vials full of incense encircle gloriously the throne of the Lamb; and side by side with them, in strange incongruity, we see figures drawn from classical antiquity, centaurs[2] and mermaids[3] and Tully[4] the philosopher, as well as dragons from Scandinavia[5], birds and monsters[6] from the mysterious East, and figures taken from contemporary life and literature.

It is possible to distinguish about twenty[7] different founts of stamps on the forty-seven bindings, which proves that the art must have been practised at many different centres; some of these were certainly in England, some certainly in France, some possibly in Germany and Scandinavia. In England alone can the bindings be localized more definitely; three[8] undoubtedly come from Winchester (see Pls. 4 and 5), since one of the three covers a cartulary of the Benedictine Monastery of St Swithin's, Winchester, and another a register of houses and property in that town; both manuscripts were written about 1150, a date which may also be assigned to the third manuscript, and to the bindings themselves. They are certainly the earliest of the English groups, and possibly the earliest of the whole Romanesque family. Their characteristics are well displayed in the example reproduced; on all three bindings some of the stamps are arranged in circles; the number of different stamps used is comparatively small, not more than sixteen or seventeen in all as compared with thirty in another group[9]

1 All these Biblical types, except the Virgin, appear in the fount used by the binder of the Pembroke Ezechiel: see Appendix E. The Virgin is found in Section L of my list only.

2 Centaurs—always with bow and arrow, and probably derived from the sign of the Zodiac Sagittarius—are found in Classes K (Nos. I and XLI), N, O (No. II) and P (No. XIX); in sculpture they may be seen, not always, though usually, with bow and arrows, on Irish crosses at Monasterboice and Kells (J. Romilly Allen, *Early Christian Symbolism in Great Britain and Ireland*, 1887, pp. 136 and 229, and H. S. Crawford, *Handbook of Carved Ornament from Irish Monuments of the Christian Period*, Dublin, 1926, Pls. XXXIX and XL); on tympana at Kencott, Salford, Stoke-sub-Hampden and Cormac's Chapel, Rock of Cashel (C. E. Keyser, *Norman tympana and lintels*, 1927, figs. 24, 69 and 70; Allen, op. cit. p. 364, n.); on fonts at West Rounton, Darenth and Hook Norton (Allen, op. cit. p. 361 and p. 364, n. 2); on columns at Adel, Tutbury and Iffley (Allen, op. cit. p. 363) and at various other places (Allen, pp. 364–5); also on an ivory box in the Victoria and Albert Museum (Miss M. H. Longhurst, *English Ivories*, n.d. Pl. XXXIII). In Scotland, centaurs carrying two axes are displayed at Aberlemno, Glamis and Meigle (J. Romilly Allen, *The Early Christian Monuments of Scotland*, 1903, Pl. I, p. 71). I quote British and Irish examples only, not later than the 12th century. The centaur at Darenth is remarkably like the stamp on No. XIX (see Pl. 29).

3 Mermaids are found in Classes F, G, H, K (No. XLI); on them see Emile Mâle, *L'Art religieux du XIIe siècle en France*, Paris, 1924, p. 335; lists of some English examples are given by Keyser, op. cit. p. 1; and Romilly Allen, op. cit. p. 368. Mâle thinks that both centaurs and mermaids are taken from the Bestiaries.

4 Of Cicero, indeed, I can quote only one sculptured representation and that is not identifiable with complete certainty. This is a figure accompanying Rhetoric, in a series of the liberal arts and their chief exponents, on the right-hand door of the west front of Chartres; but though Cicero is the most probable representative of Rhetoric, there are no attributes to put the identification beyond doubt (M. and E. Marriage, *The Sculptures of Chartres Cathedral*, Cambridge, 1909, pp. 72–3). It appears, however, from a contemporary description that Cicero was shown with other philosophers in a now-destroyed tapestry, which was presented in 1193 by the Emperor Henry VI to Cardinal Pietro da Piacenza (F. Novati, *Freschi e mini del dugento*, Milan, 1925, p. 347). A labelled stamp of Tullius is used in Class H.

5 Dragons are regarded as a sign of Norse influence by Messrs Prior and Gardner, *An Account of Medieval Figure-Sculpture in England*, Cambridge, 1912, pp. 129 and 148.

6 At least one of the formal ornaments, also, has an Eastern origin—namely stamp 44, Pl. XXVII of Dr Birkenmajer's Polish Essay, which is derived from Arabic script. There are some carved wood ornaments taken from the same source on a door in the Cathedral of Notre-Dame du Puy-en-Velay, also borders in various French and English manuscripts (see two articles by Mr Archibald H. Christie in the *Burlington Magazine* for June and July 1922).

7 See the list on p. 32.

8 Nos. V, XXI and XXII.

9 I refer to the Clairvaux β group, Class G.

also consisting of three bindings, and fifty-one noted by Weale on the four volumes of a Bible at Durham. Some of the types of stamp are found in other groups—such as the lobe-shaped[1] dragon, the bird and the curve[2], the two man-headed birds[3], the feeding ram (which elsewhere becomes a tiger[4]), the running stag[5], and some other stamps[6] not shown in the reproductions; others are peculiar to Winchester, such as the curved ornament and the foliated goat[7].

The next English group also contains three bindings, certainly executed in London about 1185 (Pls. 6, 7 and 8), since one of them covers a register of the Templars, another a manuscript which belonged to St Mary's Church, Southwark, both written about that date. Several of the stamp-types found on these London bindings are peculiar to them, for example two triangular stamps, one representing a crane[8], the other a heron killing a fish, which are curious as being almost the only triangular stamps found on any of the forty-seven bindings; or again the circular griffin, which is not unlike a griffin[9] shown on the reverse of the seal[10] of Roger de Lacy, Constable of Chester, which is taken from a document dated 1191; or most characteristic of all, the large lobe-shaped stamp of two monsters facing each other on either side of a tree, a peculiar treatment of a very ancient decorative motive, which is found in Assyrian, Persian, Greek and early[11]

1 The commonest type of stamp found on these bindings: see Appendix E, stamp No. 10.

2 Found in Classes C, F, G, H and K (No. XLI); this is one of the types that survived till the 15th century: see post, p. 17.

3 Found in Classes F and G.

4 In Classes C, F and H; there has been some controversy regarding the animal represented by these stamps; Mr G. C. Druce identifies it as a tiger, referring to 12th and 13th century Bestiaries, a misericord in Chester Cathedral, and a boss at Queen Camel in Somerset. Anyhow, there is no doubt about the identity of the ram, which is probably the sign of the Zodiac. I may add that signs of the Zodiac are common in Romanesque decoration; in England we find them at St Margaret's Walmgate, York, Kilpeck, Patrixbourne, Brimsop, Rochester, Iffley, Barton-le-Street and Bishop Wilton (Allen, op. cit. pp. 321, 323 and 330, n. 1; Prior and Gardner, pp. 36 and 194–5); they are, no doubt, equally common abroad, but I have no extended list and can quote only Toulouse, St Iago de Compostella, St Evroult de Montfort, and the Church of St Lazare, Autun (Prior and Gardner, p. 35; de Caumont, *Abécédaire d'archéologie*, Vol. II, p. 309; V. Terret, *La sculpture bourguignonne*, Autun, 1925, Vol. I, Pls. 40–6).

5 Variants in Classes E, H, K (No. XLI) and P (Nos. XIX and XXVI). The stag in Class K (No. I) (Weale and Taylor, Pl. I, No. 9) is a different type.

6 E.g.

1. Two savages with club and buckler (on No. XXII), similar stamps in Classes F and G (Birkenmajer, Pl. XXVI, figs. 23 and 24).

2. A lion sejant (on No. XXI; Weale and Taylor, Pl. I, No. 11); similar stamps in Classes F (Birkenmajer, Pl. XXVII, No. 43), H (see Pl. 16), P (see Pl. 29).

3. Two birds addorsed (on No. XXI; Weale and Taylor, Pl. I, No. 12); an almost identical stamp in Class P (see Pl. 30); similar birds, but affrontés, instead of addorsed, are found in Classes F (Birkenmajer, Pl. XXVII, No. 37) and O (No. XXVII, Gottlieb, Pl. 32). Sculptured birds in foliage, closely resembling the stamps, may be seen at Saint-Sernin, Toulouse, and Gaillac (Tarn); see R. de Lasteyrie, *L'Architecture religieuse en France à l'époque romane*, Paris, 1912, pp. 681 and 710.

7 Possibly Capricornus, the sign of the Zodiac.

8 This is probably the stamp referred to by Duff in his Sandars Lecture on *The Printers, etc. of Westminster and London*, Cambridge, 1906, p. 105; he states there that Caxton's triangular dragon stamp (shown on Pl. 42) is an exact copy of a stamp used by a London binder about the end of the 12th century. Duff probably wrote from memory; apart from their shape, the stamps have little in common, as will be seen from a comparison of Pl. 42 and Pl. 8. As I have remarked later (p. 19) and demonstrated elsewhere (*Bindings in Cambridge Libraries*, p. 30), the true affinities of Caxton's dragon stamp are some contemporary stamps used at Bruges and Ghent; but a stamp not unlike the two triangular Romanesque stamps was used at Oxford in the 15th century (see post, p. 17).

9 Griffins are not uncommon in Romanesque art; they may be seen in one of Suger's windows at St-Denis (F. de Lasteyrie, *Histoire de la peinture sur verre*, Paris, 1853, Vol. II, Pls. VI and VII), and there are fine sculptured specimens in the Musée Archéologique at Angoulême (P. Vitry and G. Brière, *Documents de sculpture française du Moyen Age*, Pl. XXI) and on the Cathedral at Borgo San Donnino (A. Venturi, *Storia dell' arte italiana*, Vol. III, Milan, 1904, fig. 128, p. 150).

10 The reproduction is from a cast in the collection of the Society of Antiquaries, London; there is another fine griffin on the seal of Duncan, son of Gilbert, Earl of Carrick, 1180 (reproduced by W. de Gray Birch, *Seals*, 1907, Pl. XXII, No. 8).

11 H. S. Crawford, op. cit. p. 65, No. 121. Mâle, pp. 346 et seq.

Irish art. Very oriental in appearance is the lion, which resembles one woven in the so-called tunic of the Virgin preserved at Chartres, a fabric now said by experts to be of Syrian[1] workmanship.

To this lion there is a parallel on the bindings of the third English group (Pl. 9), which consists in the four volumes of a huge illustrated Bible[2] written for Hugh de Puiset, Bishop of Durham, and presented by him to the Cathedral Library, Durham, where they still remain. These are the only four of the seven Romanesque bindings in that library which I believe to be of local workmanship, but there need be no hesitation in assigning these to Durham, since all the associations of the manuscript are with that city and no other works by this binder are found elsewhere. As I have said, fifty-one stamps, none very distinctive, are used on these four volumes, which probably date from about 1190, the approximate date assigned to the manuscript.

So far, we have been on fairly well-trodden ground; less familiar is the possibility that Romanesque bindings may have been produced at three English centres besides those already named. But the evidence for none is conclusive, and the evidence in favour of the first of them, Oxford, is, I regret to say, particularly weak, though it is true that *a priori* there is something to be said for the attribution. For in the 15th century University towns, and Oxford not least of them, were great centres of production of stamped bindings; what is true of the 15th century may be true also of the 12th; and in the 12th century, for some unknown reason, as a Cambridge writer amiably remarks, a University was founded at Oxford, where a conveyance of land was witnessed by a bookbinder[3] about 1180. On some of the 15th-century Oxford bindings is used a stamp of a swan passant found on the Romanesque binding reproduced (see Pls. 10 and 11). Five other stamps, of 12th-century design, and probably of 12th-century workmanship, are found on Oxford 15th-century bindings[4], and though of course they may have been engraved there or taken there at a later date, it seems more likely that they were used there in the 12th century, and that they spent the intervening years in some academic cupboard till they were roused from their long repose and set to work again when the demand for stamped leather bindings revived after the introduction of printing.

More cogent is the evidence in favour of another centre, though it consists only in a single fact—the recent discovery by the Duke of Rutland of an early binding stamp[5] at Belvoir. The stamp represents a bird-footed quadruped springing to the right in front of a conventional tree and is not unlike one used on a 13th-century binding[6] at Durham (Pl. 31). Stylistically, the stamp belongs to an early period, and it seems possible that stamped bindings may

[1] Mâle, fig. 199, p. 345; similar lions are found in the Bestiaries; see the Peterborough Psalter and Bestiary, published for the Roxburghe Club, 1921, fol. 189 b. Possibly the lion is merely the sign of the Zodiac.

[2] This is probably the most fully illustrated manuscript in any of these bindings: see E. G. Millar, *La miniature anglaise du Xe au XIIIe siècle*, Paris and Brussels, 1926, pp. 42–3 and Pl. 50.

[3] *Early Oxford Bindings*, by Strickland Gibson, 1903, p. 1; this man, Laurencius ligator, was the tenant of property in Cat Street; there is nothing to show that he produced decorated bindings.

[4] See post, pp. 16, 17.

[5] I am indebted to the Duke of Rutland and to the Council of the Society of Antiquaries for permission to reproduce this stamp, which was published in the *Antiquaries Journal*, Vol. IV, No. 3, July 1924, p. 272.

[6] A much closer parallel will be found on Pl. 19, and an attempt to interpret the stamp in Appendix D. The Durham binding is discussed in Appendix C.

have been produced in the 12th or 13th century either at Belvoir Priory where the stamp was found, or at its parent house, St Albans Abbey, which, it is hardly necessary to say, was one of the greatest literary and artistic centres in England in the 13th century.

Finally it seems far from improbable that some Romanesque bindings come from Canterbury, which was a home of English learning at this early period, and housed two of our largest libraries[1]. The manuscripts contained in some of these bindings are held by experts to have been written at Canterbury; one manuscript (No. XXXV), which certainly belonged to St Augustine's Abbey there, has been rebound; but we know from engravings of some of the stamps in Dibdin's *Bibliographical Decameron* that it was formerly in a Romanesque binding;

and Canterbury was one of the very few places in England where stamped bindings were produced in the 15th century, before the introduction of printing into this country. But whether or no Romanesque bindings were executed at either Canterbury, St Albans or Oxford, it is almost certain *a priori* that their production was not confined to the three towns, examples of whose work happen to survive—Winchester, London and Durham.

When we turn to the bindings that are certainly French, we have to deal first with a group of seven bindings[2] by two closely connected binders, which may be called the Clairvaux group, since two of the four bindings by the first craftsman and two of the three by the second belonged to that great Cistercian monastery. Their style is well shown by the two specimens illustrated (Pls. 12 to 15);

[1] Those of Christ Church Priory and St Augustine's Abbey; see Dr M. R. James, *The Ancient Libraries of Canterbury and Dover*, Cambridge, 1903. Nor should the influence of Archbishop Theobald (ob. 1161) be forgotten; he was a lover of learning, who took care to be surrounded by learned men; his palace was the training college and home of scholars and statesmen; see the *D.N.B.*

[2] Classes F and G of the list in Appendix B; in addition, Nos. XLI and XLIV belonged to Clairvaux, which therefore owned no less than six of the surviving Romanesque bindings.

it will be seen that they differ from the English bindings by the liberal and effective use of 'plait' stamps[1]; by the mermaid stamp probably derived from some Bestiary; by the number of religious figures and emblems; and by a series of stamps representing bare-headed horsemen brandishing swords. Three of the seven bindings[2]—two by the first binder, one by the second—contain the somewhat enigmatic inscription, "Henricus Regis Filius" (*vide* p. 6), and from this inscription four conclusions have been drawn:

1. That Henry the King's son was Henry, son of Louis VI of France, who was born about 1121, and died in 1175. This seems indisputable; the only rival claimant, Henry, son of our King Henry II, a brainless young ruffian, had no connection with Clairvaux, and probably never either owned[3] or opened a book during a life, the brevity of which was its only merit. Henry of France, on the other hand, entered the Church as a boy, and though not more than 15 or 16 years old at his father's death in 1137, was already Abbot of seven monasteries[4] near Paris. In 1146 the young pluralist visited Clairvaux on business, was converted by St Bernard, renounced his offices, and became a monk there, even condescending to wash dishes in the kitchen[5] of the monastery. In 1149 he was made Bishop of Beauvais and in 1162 Archbishop of Reims. We cannot be wrong in regarding him as the "Henricus Regis Filius" of the inscriptions.

2. That he gave the books to Clairvaux. This again seems to be practically certain; the books belonged to the Prince and to the monastery, and are much more likely to have passed from one to the other by gift than in any other fashion.

3. That Henry owned the books before 1137, because after his father's death, when his brother Louis VII succeeded to the throne, he became *regis frater*. This also seems probable, though not logically certain, since a king's son is always a king's son. But in documents written in the reign of Louis VII, Henry is referred[6] to as the King's brother, and the sprawling inscription looks as if he may well have written it as a schoolboy.

4. That the books were bound before 1137, or at all events before 1146, and that they were left behind at Clairvaux by Henry when he quitted the monastery in 1149. This is the crux of the whole question; for if we accept this inference, we must admit that these are the earliest of the Romanesque bindings, and therefore that the art is a

[1] By 'plait' stamps I mean the small dotted stamps used to produce an effect of plait work, as on Pls. 12 and 15.

[2] Nos. III, IV and XLII. In addition, Troyes MS. 51, Psalterium cum glossa, has the same inscription facing the title, but has been rebound; four other manuscripts at Troyes are assigned to Henry in the *Catalogue Général des MSS. des Bibliothèques des Départements*—Nos. 52 Pauli Epistolae cum glossa, 872 B Ieronimi Epistolae, 1083 Evangelium Lucae cum glossa, 1620 Epistolae Canonicae cum glossa. The attribution of these four manuscripts to Henry rests either on much later inscriptions, or merely on labels which were affixed to the bindings when the books were rebound in the 18th century; but I see no reason to doubt that all of them belonged to the Prince.

[3] Stubbs points out that great pains were taken with the education of Henry and his brothers; that Richard at all events had some literary knowledge and skill; and that John had a reputation for scholarship. But even Stubbs is unable to produce any evidence that Henry profited by instruction ('Learning and Literature at the Court of Henry II', in *Seventeen Lectures on... Medieval and Modern History*, Oxford, 1886, p. 122). Professor F. M. Powicke tells us that in 1208 John "got together or borrowed a select theological library, though unfortunately we do not know what use he and his advisers made of it" (*Stephen Langton*, Oxford, 1928, p. 99); no such story is told of Henry.

[4] St-Mellon de Pontoise, Notre-Dame de Poissi, Saint-Denis de la Châtre, Notre-Dame d'Estampes, Notre-Dame de Mantes, Notre-Dame de Corbeil, Saint-Spire de Corbeil (A. Luchaire, *Louis VI*, pp. CLIV and CLV).

[5] Letter from Eugenius III to Louis VII quoted by Dr G. G. Coulton, *Five Centuries of Religion*, Cambridge, 1923, Vol. I, p. 306.

[6] One is quoted by Dr Birkenmajer, *Jahrbuch der Einbandkunst*, Leipzig, 1927, p. 7, n. 21; another is given in Migne, *Patrologia Latina*, Vol. 185, col. 330.

French invention, brought to England probably by French workmen, under the auspices of the French prelates—Henry of Blois, Bishop of Winchester, and Hugh de Puiset, Bishop of Durham. Fortunately, there is no need to admit that these bindings are of such an early date[1], and all the circumstantial evidence is against it; everything suggests that they are not much earlier than 1170—or 1160 at earliest—and therefore that they are later than the Winchester group, which as I said may be dated 1150. The style of the stamps themselves, their relation to other founts of Romanesque stamps, and the history of Clairvaux all lead to this conclusion. To take these points in order:

The stamps used on the Clairvaux bindings, like all the other Romanesque stamps, are no doubt the work of seal cutters, and several of them recall designs found on seals. The seated king (see Pl. 14) resembles royal seals[2]; the mounted swordsmen suggest the figures found on knightly seals; and a series of architectural stamps used on bindings[3] closely allied to the Clairvaux group is clearly copied from the reverses of monastic seals[4]. Seals are valuable evidence, because they can often be dated within narrow limits; and these binding stamps will be found, on comparison, to be greatly superior to the products of the early 12th century; before 1150 seals are very crude, and generally speaking it is not till the second half of the 12th century that they are equal in workmanship to the Clairvaux stamps, which therefore would seem also to belong to the latter half of the century.

If next we compare the Clairvaux stamps with those used at Winchester, it will appear probable that the English fount is the earlier. In the first place, it is much the smaller, consisting of about seventeen stamps only, against about thirty each used by the two Clairvaux binders. That the French and English founts are not wholly independent is proved by the fact that several types of stamp[5] are common to both. But, if the Winchester craftsman be the copyist, why has he not adopted any of the useful little plait stamps? and still more curious, why has he omitted all the religious stamps—St Peter and St Paul, the emblems of the Four Evangelists[6], David with his harp, the Elders of the Apocalypse and the rest? This alone makes it almost impossible to believe in the priority of the Clairvaux fount, for such a sequence is hardly credible

[1] My thesis, as will be gathered, is that these manuscripts may have belonged to Henry, and that he may have written his name in them, long before they were bound; in support of this, apart from the arguments given in the text, is the unquestionable fact that manuscripts were sometimes left unbound for years in the Middle Ages (see Appendix K). Against it is the fact that in one MS. the words come on the liner of one of the covers, suggesting that the book was bound before the inscription was written (*Jahrbuch*, ut cit. p. 7). I do not think that this objection is wholly insuperable; the liner on which the words are written may have been originally a vellum wrapper; but even if it has to be admitted that the binding precedes the inscription, I suggest that the wording of the latter may be accounted for by supposing it to be written by Henry himself. He may well have described himself to the end of his life as 'a king's son', while others would more naturally allude to his ecclesiastical dignities or to his relationship to the reigning monarch.

[2] In general appearance, though not in detail. No great seal, either French or English, shows the king holding both sword and sceptre, nor is the latter surmounted by a simple fleur-de-lis except on the seal of the Empress Matilda of England, 1141–3 (A. B. and A. Wyon, *The Great Seals of England*, 1887, Pl. IV, fig. 29); though French seals from Louis VII to Louis VIII, 1137–1226, terminate in a fleur-de-lis within a lozenge (G. Demay, *Le Costume au moyen âge d'après les sceaux*, Paris, 1880, p. 84 and fig. 24); but the sceptres on coins often terminate in a simple fleur-de-lis (see G. C. Brooke, *A Catalogue of English Coins in the B.M.*, *The Norman Kings*, Vol. I, 1916, Pl. LXI, etc.). The throne in the stamp recalls the second seal of Richard I, c. 1197–9, more than any French seals (Wyon, Pl. VI, fig. 38; Demay, pp. 86–7).

[3] Nos. I, XXV and XXIX.

[4] Many seals of this type are in the collection of the Society of Antiquaries, London; for reproductions of 12th-century English examples see W. de G. Birch, *Catalogue of Seals in the Dept. of MSS. in the British Museum*, Vol. I, Pl. X (seals of Battle Abbey, Christ Church Priory Canterbury, Chertsey Abbey, Llandaff Chapter, Ankerwyke Priory); for a Scottish specimen, see Vol. IV, Pl. VIII (Edinburgh)

[5] See ante, p. 4, n. 1, 2, 3, 4 and 6.

[6] Weale tentatively identifies one of the stamps on No. XXI as the ox of St Luke; but the impressions are very faint, and I doubt if he is right; anyhow, one stamp does not affect my argument.

in the century which separates Hildebrand from Innocent III, a century during which the Church was steadily strengthening her hold on every kind of human endeavour and not least on the arts. It is far more likely that the Clairvaux stamp cutter borrowed some of his designs from Winchester and combined them with others taken from other sources.

Equally instructive is a comparison of the Clairvaux bindings with four[1] closely allied specimens by another binder, all of which are now in central European libraries—one at Halberstadt, one at Prague, and two, one of which is reproduced[2] (Pl. 16), in the Benedictine monastery of Admont, in Styria. It is certain that these four bindings belong to the latter half of the 12th century; the manuscript contained in one of them is definitely assigned to that period by Dr Haseloff, and one of the riders on the binding shown wears a rowel spur—a type of which the earliest representation hitherto known occurs on the seal of Jean de Boury attached to a document dated 1211[3]. This stamp can hardly have been cut over sixty years before that date; we are being generous if we concede that it may be as much as thirty years earlier. This binding and its fellows are so like the Clairvaux group that there cannot be many years between them, and this too helps to strengthen the conviction that the Clairvaux bindings also belong to the latter half[4] of the 12th century.

And it may fairly be doubted whether these bindings would have been accepted if they had been offered to Clairvaux before 1150. For the Cistercians were then in the first fine careful rapture of their Puritan enthusiasm, and ecclesiastical art of all kinds was regarded by them with suspicion. Their Consuetudines[5], promulgated in 1134, prohibit gold book clasps, painted initial letters, stained glass windows, pictures and sculpture in churches. St Bernard himself objected to tessellated pavements, wore a cotton chasuble[6], and denounced sculptured ornament in cloisters, in a passage which might be applied almost unchanged to these Romanesque bindings[7]. "What profit is there", he asks, "in those ridiculous monsters, in that marvellous and deformed comeliness, that comely deformity? To what purpose are those unclean apes, those fierce lions, those monstrous centaurs, those half men, those striped tigers, those fighting knights[8], those hunters winding their horns? Many bodies are there seen

[1] Nos. XXV, XXIX, XXXVI and XXXIX—Class H.

[2] The stamp shown in two horizontal rows on the central portion of the lower cover of this binding is exceedingly curious, and I can suggest no very satisfactory explanation of it. But it seems to me possible that the two little figures may come from a series of groups representing the nations of the world to whom the Gospel is being preached, such as may be seen at Vézelay (Mâle, op. cit. pp. 326–31).

[3] G. Demay, op. cit. fig. 140; the type was comparatively rare throughout the 13th century, the second example quoted by Demay being taken from a document dated 1228, the third from one of 1237, the fourth from one of 1246; it is not till the 14th century that rowels come into general use. In England they do not appear before the second seal of Henry III in 1240 (Sir Guy Laking, *European Armour and Arms*, Vol. I, p. 106, and Vol. III, p. 164). The 9th-century example quoted by Victor Gay, *Glossaire archéologique*, Paris, 1887, art. Éperon, rests on evidence far too slight to be acceptable.

[4] It seems quite possible that the analogous bindings (Class H) are later still; one of the stamps found on them—a lobe-shaped double-headed eagle (reproduced *Jahrbuch*, Tafel 4, No. 12)—is very closely allied to a stamp on No. XXXV (see p. 6), and the manuscript once contained in the latter binding is assigned by Mr J. A. Herbert to the 13th century; cf. also Pls. 18 and 31.

[5] Ph. Guignard, *Les monuments primitifs de la règle cistercienne*, Dijon, 1878, pp. 253, 255 and 272.

[6] Dr G. G. Coulton, *Five Centuries of Religion*, Vol. I, Cambridge, 1923, p. 281.

[7] I quote the version given by Dr Coulton, *A Medieval Garner*, p. 72.

[8] Two fine stamps of tilting knights on No. XXXI; the best known sculptured knights of this period are on the Cathedral at Angoulême (Mâle, fig. 230); in England we find them at Barfreston in Kent (Prior and Gardner, figs. 175–6) and at Brayton, near Selby in Yorkshire (*The Reliquary*, Vol. II, N.S. 1888, Pl. XXII). Mr A.

under one head, or again, many heads to a single body. Here is a four-footed beast, with a serpent's tail; there a fish with a beast's head. Here again the forepart of a horse trails half a goat behind it, or a horned beast bears the hinder quarters of a horse. In short, so many and so marvellous are the varieties of divers shapes on every hand, that we are more tempted to read in the marble than in our books, and to spend the whole day in wondering at these things rather than in meditating the law of God. For God's sake, if men are not ashamed of these follies, why at least do they not shrink from the expense?"

No doubt these ascetic ideals were soon abandoned, but there can have been little serious departure from them at Clairvaux before the death of St Bernard in 1153. The manuscripts therefore were probably bound for Archbishop Henry towards the close of his life, and given by the weary prelate to Clairvaux in memory of the carefree days which he had spent there long before.

Unless the bindings are the work of itinerant craftsmen, which is possible, it is unlikely that they were executed at Clairvaux itself; first because they are the work of two binders using wholly different founts of tools, secondly because both binders worked for other patrons; two bindings by the first (Nos. XX and XXX) and one by the second binder (No. XXXIV) are known which never belonged either to Henry or to Clairvaux; possibly both binders were monks in other monasteries which made a practice of producing these stamped bindings.

French also are two bindings by different craftsmen who seem to have patronized the same stamp cutter, a second rate imitator of the man who supplied the Clairvaux binders. One of these (No. XLI, Pl. 17)[1] was given to that monastery by John of Pisa, Canon of Laon, and is now in the Town Library of Troyes, to which most of the Clairvaux manuscripts were transferred at the French Revolution. The other (No. I), in the British Museum, was thought by Weale to be the earliest of the whole Romanesque family, no doubt because of the crudity of its ornaments; but bad workmen are at home in all periods and the stamps are as likely to be degenerate as primitive.

Leaving the bindings which I regard as undoubtedly French, we come to a group which is of uncertain origin. At least four, and possibly six, different craftsmen are responsible for the fourteen bindings which compose it (Classes L to P); five of them have been in England from an early period, the rest belong to the Continent, two being in France, one in Spain, four in Germany, and one in Poland; one (No. II), which is now in the British Museum, belonged in the 15th century to the monastery

Kingsley Porter discusses the motive in his very comprehensive work, *Romanesque Sculpture of the Pilgrimage Roads*, 10 vols, Boston, U.S.A., 1923, Vol. I, pp. 64–5, and suggests that it is more at home in Italy or Spain than in the north; but he does not mention the English examples. Of the other motives denounced by St Bernard, lions are found in several groups (see p. 4, n. 6 and p. 5) and so are centaurs (see p. 3, n. 2), half men with shields are also common (see Appendix E, stamp 34), tigers may possibly be seen in Classes F and H (see p. 4, n. 4), a putative hunter on No. XLIII (see Pl. 18).

[1] As will be seen, this binding is in poor condition; the lower cover indeed is so badly damaged that it is impossible to reproduce it satisfactorily; the stamps on it that I can identify are:

1. Two man-headed birds: see p. 4, n. 3.
2. A palmette: see Appendix E, stamp No. 12.
3. A mermaid: see p. 3, n. 3.
4. Large bird passant to sinister: see Appendix E, stamp No. 28.
5. A small roundel.

Some of the stamps on this binding may be those used in Class F: the condition of the binding is too bad for certainty on this point to be possible.

of St Paul at Erfurt. But widely scattered as they are, they can be grouped together, for through them all runs the work of a stamp cutter of genius who has thrown over the whole family of Romanesque bindings a glamour which perhaps it does not wholly deserve. Most of his stamps belong to the usual types; but he had a fondness for two-headed grotesques, one of which represents the two-headed serpent or amphisbaena[1] beloved by medieval artists; the rest—four in number—are half human, half animal, but all full of life and rhythm and character.

The first bindery of the group (see Pls. 20, 21 and 21 *a* and *b*) seems to have employed this great artist alone, and the superiority of his stamps to those of his contemporaries is very marked, though the binders unfortunately did not know how to make a very good use of them. Contrast the kneeling Elder and the mounted King bearing a palm branch with their counterparts on the excellent Clairvaux binding reproduced in Pl. 14; how lifeless and wooden is the Frenchman's work compared with that of the great unknown, though the Clairvaux binder knew how to use his stamps much better than his contemporary. The bindings in this section (L) are five in number—two at Durham, one at Hereford, one at Lambach in Austria, and the last at Vich in Catalonia. They are all very similar in design, but the Hereford binding has an interesting stamp of the Last Supper, not found on any of the others; some use is made of plait stamps in this section, though far less than on the Clairvaux bindings.

The next section[2] is of peculiar interest here, for to it belongs the only Romanesque binding in Cambridge, on a glossed manuscript of Ezechiel in the Library of Pembroke College. In this section we find none of the stamps of the first section, but we find others which are certainly by the great unknown artist, side by side with stamps of very inferior quality which are obviously by another hand. On the first binding shown (Pls. 22 and 23), it is true, we seem to have the stamps of the great man only, including two other grotesques; but on the Pembroke binding (Pls. 26 and 27) a very inferior craftsman is represented whose stamp of Samson and the Lion is an uncouth and clumsy caricature of the great master's version. The five bindings in this section (M) are divided between England, France and Poland. I class with these two sections a binding in the British Museum (No. II) and another at Vienna (No. XXVII), because each has a different grotesque of the same two-headed type; also two bindings at Admont in Styria (Nos. XXXVII and XXXVIII—see Pl. 28), because they alone share stamps of the Holy Dove and of a seated king with foliage, which both come from a Jesse tree—types found in the section to which the Pembroke Ezechiel[3] belongs.

It is, I think, certain that all the different sections of this doubtful group came into existence not far from the Straits of Dover, in South-East England or in Northern France, and it is quite possible that they should be divided between the two shores of the Channel. The Pembroke manuscript is thought by experts to have been written at Canterbury[4], and if this be so there seems to be no reason to suppose that it has ever been out of England. A very beautiful stamp of a six-foiled flower[5], used on one of the bindings in the same section, has an almost ludicrously exact counterpart in carved stone ornaments on the Norman churches of Great Washbourn in Gloucestershire and Bredwardine in Herefordshire.

[1] See Appendix E, stamps 6 and 7.

[2] See Appendix E for a list of the stamps in this section.

[3] See Appendix E, stamps 4 and 25.

[4] *Jahrbuch*, p. 13, n. 6.

[5] See Appendix E, stamp 29.

But there are also links with France[1]. In particular, several types of stamp, not found on any of the English bindings, are common to both the French and the doubtful groups: such as the kneeling Elder, the mounted King carrying a palm branch[2], the ecclesiastic[3], the running dog[4], and the very curious stamp of a mounted swordsman issuing from an archway[5]. This stamp is of considerable interest, for there is a similar figure on the Porta della Pescheria of the Cathedral at Modena, and from an inscription which accompanies it there is no doubt that it is taken from the Arthurian legend, and represents the giant Carradoc sallying from his castle. The figure is very rare in Romanesque art, and its presence on both groups of bindings, combined with the other coincidences, proves pretty clearly the close relationship between them.

Two isolated bindings may be mentioned as both have features of special interest: one (No. XIX, Pls. 29 and 30), which is now in the British Museum, belonged previously to two English collectors, Sir Thomas Phillipps and George Dunn; it may be of English workmanship, since the manuscript which it covers is thought to have been for the most part[6] written in England. It is noteworthy as being the only Romanesque binding composed entirely of leather[7], without wooden boards; thirteen stamps are used on it, belonging mainly to the Winchester and Clairvaux types. The other binding (No. XXXI) is in the University Library at Basle, and covers a manuscript assigned to the second half of the 13th century; but the stamps must be of much earlier date, since one of them represents a mounted knight wearing the conical helmet and long hauberk of the 12th century.

There is but scanty evidence that Romanesque bindings of any merit were produced outside France and England. Dr Birkenmajer discovered at Halberstadt[8] what is certainly a German stamped binding of the period, but the tools are few and coarse and the workmanship clumsy. It is true that nearly one-third of all the surviving Romanesque bindings are in Central or Eastern European libraries, and it is interesting to observe that some 12th-century stamps were closely imitated by Bavarian and Westphalian[9] binders in the 15th century. But both facts may be accounted for by supposing that French bindings were taken home in the 12th century by some of the German students who thronged to the schools for which Northern France was noted at the time, not only at Paris but also at Chartres, Reims, Laon, Tours, and especially Orleans[10], where, it is said, German rang in the streets as in the Fatherland.

[1] See Appendix F for a fuller discussion of the nationality of the doubtful group.

[2] See Appendix E, stamp No. 5.

[3] On Nos. I and XLI (Class K) and XXXVIII (Class N).

[4] See Appendix E, stamp No. 19.

[5] Used on Nos. XXVII and XXXII only in the doubtful group; also in Class H. Dr Haseloff pointed out the resemblance between this stamp and the sculpture on the archivolt of the Porta dei Leoni of S. Nicola at Bari (*Miscellanea Francesco Ehrle*, Vol. V, p. 523). On the two sculptures see Mâle, op. cit. fig. 176, pp. 268–9, and A. Kingsley Porter, op. cit. Vol. I, pp. 62–3.

[6] See the *Catalogue of additions to the MSS. in the British Museum*, 1911–15, p. 413.

[7] Several bindings of this type are mentioned in the catalogue of the Louvre Library made in 1373 by Gilles Mallet (published by De Bure, Paris, 1836); e.g. No. 823 'Couvert de noir sans aiz', No. 824 'Couvert de rouge sans aiz'.

[8] *Jahrbuch*, p. 20; later another very similar binding was found at Leipzig and reproduced by Dr Glauning; see No. XLV.

[9] See my contribution to *Jahrbuch*, II.

[10] Helen Waddell, *The Wandering Scholars*, London, 1927, p. 216.

Finally, there comes an interesting piece of evidence from Denmark—a small oblong stamp of a dragon[1], found in the ruins of the castle of Lilleborg on the Island of Bornholm. The stamp cannot be later than 1259, as the castle was burnt down in that year, and it is probably a good deal earlier; it is not the right shape for a seal and is unlikely to have been used by anybody but a worker in leather; it is possible, therefore, that decorated leather bindings were executed in Scandinavia before the middle of the 13th century[2].

[1] I am greatly indebted to the Curator of the National Museum (2. Afdeling), Copenhagen, for sending me an electrotype of this very interesting stamp and permitting me to reproduce it. Unlike the Belvoir stamp, it has no handle or tang but only a little hole drilled in one end.

[2] It is possible that we owe the stamp to an English craftsman, or at all events to English inspiration. Matthew Paris records that Anketil, a metalworker and monk of St Albans, worked for a time in Denmark (quoted by Mr O. M. Dalton, *British Museum, A Guide to the Medieval Antiquities*, 1924, p. 190). On the other hand, Denmark at the end of the 12th century was feeling the full influence of French manners, art and scholarship (F. M. Powicke, *The Loss of Normandy*, Manchester, 1913, p. 138).

II

The Gothic Bindings, c. 1450–1500

BEFORE CONSIDERING IN DETAIL OUR LATE GOTHIC bindings, I should like to call attention to two very marked differences between them and the Romanesque type, which at first sight are not easy to explain. One is prepared for differences in stamps and patterns; ornament and design are not likely to remain constant during three centuries of great artistic activity and achievement; but why did the binders of the 12th century use so many more stamps than their successors in the 15th? In three Romanesque groups, the largest of which contains only five bindings, we find founts of thirty, forty-three and fifty-one stamps respectively; it is but seldom that one finds less than ten or twelve stamps on one cover, whereas five or six are a liberal allowance in the 15th century, when some covers were very adequately decorated with repetitions of a single tool[1].

The explanation, I think, lies in what political economists beautifully call 'the higgling of the market'—that is, in this case, the conflict of interests between stamp cutter and binder; the former naturally wanted to sell as many of his wares as possible; the latter, to buy no more than he really needed. The struggle was won in the 12th century by the stamp cutters, who managed to sell a great many more stamps than the binders could use effectively; in the 15th century, on the other hand, the binders were victorious, and these opposite results are readily intelligible if we remember that the early binders were monks[2], and that their stamps were bought out of the revenues of the community; whereas their successors were business men, who had to pay for their stock-in-trade themselves.

Romanesque bindings have another characteristic which distinguishes them from all later work; they have invariably two different schemes of decoration on the two covers, whereas the two covers of later bindings are generally uniform. Since man is naturally lazy, and since it obviously saves trouble to make one pattern do a double duty, I can only suppose that the early binders never thought of making the two covers alike; in this respect they imitated the handsome metal bindings which they saw in their churches, the covers of which are necessarily different, since the lower cover, on which the book rests, must be flat, while the upper cover was heavily embossed and often decorated with plates of ivory or enamel.

We have next to account if we can for the complete and sudden disappearance of Romanesque bindings; their last belated survivor cannot be much after 1250; the earliest English Gothic binding cannot be much earlier than 1450; and no surviving English stamped binding can be placed with certainty[3] in the intermediate period.

[1] E.g. most of the bindings by Caxton's first binder: see post, p. 19.

[2] Perhaps this sentence assumes rather more than it should do; it has never been formally proved that the Romanesque bindings were monastic, and I think it would be difficult to show that larger founts of stamps were used by monks than by tradesmen in the 15th century. But broadly speaking, I think it is true that in the 12th century it was the monks who set the pace, and in the 15th century the tradesmen.

[3] The one possible exception known to me is reproduced as Pl. 31. I can, however, record three pieces of English stamped leather, all probably belonging to the 14th century:

1. The mitre case of William of Wykeham (1324–1404) at New College, Oxford; reproduced in *The Connoisseur*, Jan. 1905, p. 56.

2 and 3. Two cases, for a silver basin and ewer, in the Museum of the Public Record Office (Catalogue by Sir H. C. Maxwell Lyte, 12th edition, 1926, pp. 71–2, Nos. IV and VIII); the latter reproduced in *Gleanings from Westminster Abbey*, by Gilbert Scott and others, 1863, p. 95.

All three pieces are decorated with close diapers of small fleur-de-lis stamps.

True, this is not the case everywhere; stamped leather bindings are frequently mentioned in a catalogue[1] of the library of the Louvre compiled in 1373, and several such bindings[2] are known which must be assigned to the 14th century. But even here there is a great gulf fixed; for the 14th-century bindings of which the example shown is typical (Pl. 32 b) are quite unlike earlier work; the old stamp models have disappeared and have been replaced by smaller and less interesting types, which are almost invariably massed in more or less closely set vertical rows. Stamps and designs are poor and monotonous compared with the variety and invention of the earlier period, and we may well ask how it happens that the 14th century, which produced great works of art of every kind from miniatures to cathedrals, should have left hardly anything[3] of any interest to the student of bindings.

The answer again lies in recognition of the fact that the early binders were monks and the later laymen; not that monks are necessarily, or even probably, greater artists[4] than laymen—far from it; but they had at their disposal the revenues of wealthy communities and their successors had to rely on their own resources. The monks could have their stamps cut by the best seal cutters, the laymen had to go to the cheapest. In monasteries, the art died out with the gradual waning of monastic industry after 1200; and the comparatively feeble and undeveloped book trade of the 13th century could not take its place. The revival in the 15th century was due partly to the monastic[5] reformation in Germany and the Low Countries, led by the Austin Canons of Windesheim and the Brethren of the Common Life, and partly to the great development of the book trade after the invention of printing.

To the average Englishman of that period stamped bindings must have seemed as much a foreign invention as printed books; and it is not surprising that one of the first places at which they appear should be Canterbury, the literary centre nearest to France and therefore most exposed to foreign influence. Six[6] of these Canterbury bindings (Pl. 33) are known to me, three of them, all in Bodley's Library, covering

[1] About 75 out of the 1236 books are described as being in 'cuir a empraintes' in the catalogue by Gilles Mallet, published by De Bure, 1836.

[2] Reproductions in S. Gibson, *Some Notable Bodleian Bindings*, Oxford, 1901–4, Pl. 3; Gruel, *Manuel*, Vol. I, p. 14; Gottlieb in *Belvedere*, Jan. 1926, Pl. 4; Schmidt, *Bucheinbände...zu Darmstadt*, 1921, Pl. 1; *Loubier Festschrift*, Pl. 14. Mr E. P. Goldschmidt's specimen (No. 40) is a late example of the same type; I do not know why he calls it monastic; it seems to me to be just as likely to be a trade binding.

[3] I except of course the German cut-leather bindings, which have been admirably reproduced by Dr M. Bollert, *Lederschnittbände des XIV Jahrhundert*, Leipzig, 1925. But Dr Bollert gives us plates of no more than twenty-one specimens; and several even of these, according to Dr Gottlieb, belong to the 15th century (see his review of the book in *Göttingischen gelehrten Anzeigen*, 1927, Nr. 9–10).

[4] On monks as artists see Dr G. G. Coulton, *Art and the Reformation*, Oxford, 1928, chs. II–IV.

[5] See E. P. Goldschmidt, *Gothic and Renaissance Bookbindings*, 1928, p. 7.

[6] The list is as follows:

	DATE OF THE MS.	EARLY OWNER	PRESENT OWNER	PRESSMARK OR REFERENCE
I	12th–13th century	St Augustine's Abbey, Canterbury	Bodley's Library	MS. Seld. Infra 25
II	15th century (early)	Christ Church Priory, Canterbury	Bodley's Library	MS. Bodl. 281
III	c. 1465	W. Boolde, a monk of Christ Church Priory, Canterbury	Bodley's Library	MS. Bodl. 648
IV	15th century (late)	James Goldwell, Bishop of Norwich, ob. 1499, who was a native of Kent; see the *D.N.B.*	Canon Streeter	Bodleian Quarterly Record, No. 54
V and VI	Empty Bindings	Unknown	Bodley's Library	Douce Scrapbook 112 and 124

I owe my knowledge of these bindings, and the particulars regarding them, to Mr Strickland Gibson.

manuscripts which belonged to one or other of the two great monastic libraries in Canterbury. The specimen shown is characteristic; both the stamps and the general design are very reminiscent of foreign work, though the circular ornaments and the interlacing rectangles break away from French patterns. I place these among the earliest English 15th-century stamped bindings, partly because they are very archaic in style, and partly because none covers a printed book.

Next to them may be mentioned two almost identical bindings (Pl. 34), covering manuscripts written[1] at Salisbury between 1458 and 1460 by Hermann Zurke of Griefswald for Gilbert Kymer, Dean of Salisbury, previously Chancellor of Oxford University and physician to Humphrey, Duke of Gloucester. Here again we see in the centre closely set vertical rows of small stamps, but the most prominent features of the bindings are the large mottoes—"Mon bien mondain" and "Jesu mercy lady help". The former is said to have been used by Humphrey, Duke of Gloucester, who died in 1447, and it was no doubt adopted by Kymer in memory of his patron. Large inscriptions are seldom, if ever, found on French 15th-century bindings, but they are not uncommon[2] in Germany, and it is possible that this modification of the traditional type was suggested by the scribe Hermann Zurke, who had no doubt seen something similar in his native country.

The third town in which we find this French fashion of arranging stamps in vertical rows is Oxford, which like Erfurt and many other University[3] towns was a great book-binding centre in the 15th century. Mr Strickland Gibson, in his monograph[4] on Oxford bindings, has given us much information and many reproductions both of bindings and stamps; but he has not attempted to distinguish systematically between the various binderies, and it would be impossible to do so satisfactorily without much detailed investigation. But using his book as a foundation for study, we find that ninety different stamps were used at Oxford on thirty-three 15th-century bindings; if we group together the stamps found on the same bindings and assume that none of the stamps changed hands, we shall find it necessary to postulate eleven[5] different binders. Unfortunately, the question cannot be so easily decided; eight out of the eleven binders would be represented by a single volume each, while one of the other three would have twenty-two to his credit and possess no less than forty-two stamps. Two of these twenty-two bindings are illustrated; they have neither stamps nor design in common, though they may be connected through stamps used on other bindings. None the less it seems very unlikely that the two come from the same workshop; and the probability is that some of the stamps changed hands.

The first of these two bindings (Pl. 35) is of particular interest since the four stamps used on it are all of 12th-century design, and the same binder possessed two other stamps equally archaic in appearance[6]. One of those shown, indeed, a swan passant,

[1] See S. Gibson, op. cit. Pl. 5; Weale (R. 42) assigned to Salisbury the binding of a Salisbury cartulary which he dated 1447. The pattern and stamps are of the same 'French' type, and it seems to me possible that the volume was bought as a blank notebook, and perhaps even imported from the Continent. It has no stamps in common with the Salisbury binding reproduced on Pl. 34 or its fellow.

[2] E.g. Dr M. J. Husung, *Bucheinbände aus der preussischen Staatsbibliothek*, Leipzig, 1925, p. 13, Tafel XXXI, abb. 44. On this binding each letter is stamped with a separate tool; but there are many others on which whole words are stamped together.

[3] See E. P. Goldschmidt, op. cit. pp. 44 et seq.

[4] *Early Oxford Bindings*. Printed for the Bibliographical Society of London, 1903.

[5] See Appendix G for an attempted classification of Oxford 15th-century bindings.

[6] See ante, p. 5; the six stamps are Gibson, op. cit. Nos. 1–5 and 80.

is certainly of 12th-century workmanship, being found on a binding of that period, to which I have already referred (see p. 5). Another, the curve and the bird, is taken from the same drawing as four stamps used by the Winchester, Durham and Clairvaux binders (see p. 4, n. 2); while yet another, a triangular stamp of a crane, which is not reproduced here, closely resembles two stamps used by the early London binder (see p. 4, n. 8). The other three stamps, two of which are illustrated, are thoroughly Romanesque in character, though they have no counterparts among the surviving stamps of the period—one of many reminders that the 12th-century bindings which we possess can be but a very small fraction of those produced. This binder may have been at work as early as 1460, several manuscripts of about that date in his bindings being known; the latest binding decorated with any of these archaic stamps seems to be the Register of the Holy Cross of Stratford-on-Avon which was finished in 1489.

The next binding (Pl. 36) is archaic in a different fashion; the stamps are of the 15th-century type, possibly imported from the Netherlands, but the decorative scheme follows the old Winchester model very closely and may well be imitated from it. This binding, which is in the University Library, covers a book printed at Oxford in 1482; one of the very few other 15th-century bindings known[1] with this scheme of decoration is also at Cambridge, in the Library of St John's College, but there is little evidence to connect this latter binding with Oxford, though it is claimed by Mr Gibson.

Our third Oxford binding (Pl. 37) belongs to a type always associated with the first Oxford printers, Rood and Hunte; it seems to appear first about 1478, when they started printing; the stamps and designs are certainly foreign, being of the lower Rhenish type; and the binder may well have been in the service of the two printers, and come over with them from Cologne. But, like all binders of the period, this craftsman did not restrict himself to binding the books printed by his employers, for at least one Caxton[2] and several books printed abroad survive in his bindings. He was fond of making a frame, as on the binding shown, with the foliated staff, a stamp which has a family resemblance to a type[3] used by several binders in South Germany and Northern Italy.

The same arrangement of stamps in vertical or horizontal rows was occasionally adopted by the first London[4] binder to claim our attention, and he no doubt copied it from some French or Rhenish model. But he did not by any means always follow it; and indeed his bindings are so varied and so peculiar that he is by far the most interesting English binder of his period. He alone produced covers of cut leather, in addition to those decorated with figured stamps; and he alone indicated in some way or another, on almost all his bindings, the patron by whom they were commissioned. Thus two of his bindings—one at St John's College, the other in the Rylands Library, Manchester—bear the letters L A N G and a barrel or tun; if there were any doubt

[1] Gibson, op. cit. binding No. 23, Pls. XIV and XV. Some bindings with the ornament arranged in circles were produced at St Peter's Monastery, Erfurt; *Monatshefte für Bücherfreunde*, Leipzig, 1925, pp. 397 and 400.

[2] *Description of Britain*, Bodl. S. Seld. d. 4, see Gibson, op. cit. p. 20.

[3] See *Jahrbuch*, Tafel 6, Abb. 2 and Dr A. Schmidt, *Bucheinbände... in der Landesbibliothek zu Darmstadt*, Leipzig, 1921, Pls. XII and XXII, for German examples; for Italian, see Brunet, Pl. 82; this is the binding with the arms of the Pucci family referred to by Mr E. P. Goldschmidt, p. 73. The stamp of two birds drinking from a cup shown on Pl. 37 is interesting iconographically, for like nearly all such stamps with two symmetrical birds or animals it comes originally from the East; two peacocks, drinking in very similar fashion from a vase with a long knopped stem, may be seen on a stone slab from Venice, now in the Kaiser Friedrich Museum, Berlin (reproduced by H. Glück, *Die Christliche Kunst des Ostens*, Berlin, 1923, Pl. 17). Three variants of the stamp were used at Oxford; Gibson, op. cit. stamps 41, 47 and 56.

[4] I have written at length on this binder in *Bindings in Cambridge Libraries* and reproduced five of his works.

of this being a rebus for Langton, it would be set at rest by the fact that the owner's name, W. Langton, is written in the Manchester book. He has been identified as William Langton, Chancellor, and afterwards Precentor of York, brother of the better known Thomas Langton, who died in 1501 as Archbishop-Elect of Canterbury; and it is interesting to note that Thomas Langton also was fond of rebuses, though to represent the first syllable of his name he used the musical note known as a long.

On another binding may be seen a large C and a small tun for Seton; two others are scored J.W.; others again have a capital P or a capital L; another—perhaps the most curious of all—in the Library of Corpus Christi College, has the stamps arranged in the form of a coat of arms, a device which is, so far as I know, almost[1] without parallel in the 15th century. Several bindings have a stamp bearing the words "En Dieu ma fye"; but since this is found with various indications of ownership, it would appear to be the binder's personal motto.

To his identity there is no real clue; it has been suggested that he was called Scales, since one of the stamps of which he was fondest represents a pair of scales; but this may equally well indicate the sign of his shop, or it may have been adopted in compliment to Anthony Woodville, Baron Scales, and afterwards Earl Rivers, an accomplished nobleman, who was one of Caxton's patrons, and possibly a patron of our binder also. But, whatever the latter's name, it is fairly certain that he was a London[2] leatherworker, who occasionally bound a book to the order of some favoured client. There is in the British Museum a case of cut leatherwork (Pl. 40) found in London which in quality of material, technique[3] and decoration is remarkably similar to the work of the Scales binder. Connection seems to be established by a very singular peculiarity which is common to both but shared by no other English binder—the practice namely of casually strewing the surface to be decorated with repeated impressions of a capital letter. On two of the bindings we find a capital S used in this way, and on one of the pieces of leatherwork shown on Pl. 40 we find A, B and M.

Common also to leatherworkers and binder is the practice of scoring inscriptions with a knife in Gothic letters; thus a swordbelt in the London Museum bears the words "Rive Mevynt Faste"—that is "Fasten me Fast", and on a cylindrical box belonging to Moulton Church in Norfolk, presumably intended to hold a winecup, we find the exhortation "Be Meri Mon" (see Pl. 41). Similarly on one of the Scales bindings at Trinity College (Pl. 39) is incised the word "Bhale"[4], no doubt the owner's name.

The stamps used by this binder seem to fall into two categories; some are small and finely engraved, and resemble those used by Rood and Hunte's binder; these are no doubt imported. Others are larger and coarser and were probably bought from a London stamp cutter; one of these, representing a nosegay, which is shown on Pl. 39, belongs to a type that we shall meet again more than once. The latest imprint in any known binding by this remarkable craftsman is 1481.

[1] Judging from the catalogue description, Lot 3521 of the George Dunn Library was in a similar binding.

[2] The attribution to London is, perhaps, slightly strengthened by the fact, which I discovered after delivering my lecture, that one of his stamps is not unlike the leopard's head which has been since 1300 the mark of the London Agency office. There was a goldsmith named William Scales, first mentioned in 1447, who may be connected with our binder.

[3] For English leatherwork of the later Middle Ages, see Appendix K.

[4] Compare also the four-leaved flower on this binding with the similar but smaller ornament of the same kind on the centre piece of leather reproduced on Pl. 40.

For our purposes, Westminster and London may be treated as one, and we may turn to consider the productions of a bindery which worked much for Caxton and was possibly under his roof, since several of its products are lined with his trial sheets. On these bindings we find a new pattern, certainly taken from the Low Countries; instead of the stamps being massed together in rows, a frame parallel to the edges of the boards is formed either by lines ruled with a graver, or by repetitions of a single stamp, and within this frame the field is divided into lozenge-shaped compartments, a single stamp[1] being placed in the centre of each. This pattern, which was almost universally used in England at the close of the 15th century, was probably introduced by the Caxton bindery. Its most familiar work is of the type shown (Pl. 43), which covers the British Museum copy of Caxton's[2] third edition of the *Dictes and Sayings of the Philosophers*. Among the stamps will be noticed one of a nosegay, resembling the stamp used by the Scales binder.

With the stamps illustrated is sometimes associated a triangular dragon stamp, the recurrence of which makes it possible to assign to this workshop a binding in the Library of Corpus Christi College (Pl. 42); on this the dragon is accompanied by a fleur-de-lis stamp, which is disposed over the central field in a very distinctive fashion. I know of three[3] other bindings with the same fleur-de-lis stamp, arranged in the same way, one of them on a copy of Caxton's first edition of Gower's *Confessio Amantis*, which until 1926 had been from time immemorial in an old English country-house library; but the triangular dragon occurs on the Corpus binding only, which covers a copy of the Oxford edition of Lyndewoode's *Provinciale*. The two stamps and the pattern—even the device of placing four fleurs-de-lis in the form of a cross—are all characteristic of the Netherlands and particularly of Bruges; and I have no doubt that we owe the fleur-de-lis and dragon stamps to a Bruges stamp cutter, and the bindings to a Bruges binder who came over to England either with Caxton in 1476 or very shortly afterwards. Similar stamps and a similar design will be found on bindings in the University Library and at Queens' College[4], which can be proved to come from the same workshop as a binding in Bodley's Library containing the inscription "Johannis Meese me ligavit"; the binder's real name was Guilebert, and he was a man of importance at Bruges where he worked for about twenty-four years. It is probable that these fleur-de-lis bindings are earlier than those of the better known type illustrated on Pl. 43, since the latest imprint in any of them is 1483, whereas the others continued to be produced long after Caxton's death, the latest known to me, which was formerly in Lord Mostyn's library, covering an imprint of 1510[5]. The most interesting of these later bindings (Pl. 44) is in Lincoln Cathedral Library, on a copy of Wynkyn de Worde's *Vitas Patrum*, printed in 1495; it is the only binding known to me with the small stamp of the Royal Arms, which, in this form, with a border, was used by various members of the Beaufort[6] family;

[1] Mr E. P. Goldschmidt's 'English pattern' (p. 23) is simply the 16th-century development of this arrangement, the frame being formed with a roll instead of with single tools, and 'pineapple stamps' (see post, p. 22, n. 3) being substituted for the 15th-century types. Pls. 46, 48 and 50 are good examples of the earlier period, Pls. 49 and 51 of the transition; for the fully developed 16th-century pattern, see G. J. Gray, *The Earlier Cambridge Stationers, etc.*, 1904, Pls. XIII, XIV and XVII.

[2] Pressmark I B 55143; formerly in the library of Sir J. Radcliffe, sold at Sotheby's, Dec. 15th, 1916, Lot 723.

[3] See my remarks in *Bindings in Cambridge Libraries*, Pl. XV, stamp 38.

[4] Reproduced in *Bindings in Cambridge Libraries*, Pl. X.

[5] Sold at Sotheby's, April 15th, 1920, Lot 200; reproduced in the sale catalogue.

[6] Information from Mr R. Griffin, F.S.A. and Mr A. G. B. Russell, Lancaster Herald.

whether it indicates ownership or patronage or is merely decorative I am unable to say. I may add that the characteristic stamps of what I may call the second Caxton manner, namely, the nosegays and a large lozenge-shaped griffin, seem to be South German in type; they are similar to stamps used on what are generally called Koberger's trade bindings[1], and were no doubt brought over to England by a second craftsman, possibly, like Wynkyn de Worde, a native of Alsace, who presumably superseded his brother-binder from Bruges soon after 1483.

The next London binder seems to have worked for a short time only, since his five known bindings[2] all cover books printed between 1475 and 1480. But he is notable for several reasons, the chief being that in one of the books bound by him—a two volume Bible printed at Cologne in 1480, now at Jesus College—Bradshaw found long ago the only fragments known of two Indulgences printed by John Lettou, the first London printer, in 1481. From this it has been deduced that the binding was executed by Lettou, but I do not think that the discovery proves more than that the binding is not earlier than 1481, and that it is probably of London workmanship. The example illustrated (Pl. 45) is in Lincoln Cathedral Library, and it shows all the stamps used by this binder; the two dragons with interlocking necks are a decorative motive, which goes back to ancient Babylonian[3] art, and probably came to Europe in the ornament of the woven silks which were so popular during the early Middle Ages; this stamp is very similar to one used at Oxford[4].

The other large stamp, that of a crane attacking a quadruped, is also probably of Asiatic origin. Hawking has been popular in the East from the earliest times, and animals attacked by birds of prey are common in Eastern art. This motive too came

[1] See *Jahrbuch,* Tafel 6; the nosegay is also found at Lübeck. See *Bibliografiska Studier tillägnade Friherre Johannes Rudbeck,* Stockholm, 1917, p. 16. A list of the stamps owned by the Caxton binders may be useful, but it is probably incomplete, as I do not know the Caxtons in America:

	DESCRIPTION	SHAPE	REPRODUCTION
1	Fleur-de-lis	'Free' (see below)	See Pl. 42; *Bindings in Cambridge Libraries,* Pl. XV, stamp 38
2	Dragon	Triangular	See Pl. 42; *Bindings in Cambridge Libraries,* Pl. X, dragon 19
3	Griffin[5]	Lozenge	W. Y. Fletcher, *English Bindings in the British Museum,* Pl. III
4	Carrot ? or opening bud?	Do	Fletcher, ut cit.
5	Foliated square	Do.	E. G. Duff, *William Caxton,* Chicago, 1905, frontispiece
6 & 7	Two nosegays	Do.	See Pls. 43 and 44
8	Beaufort Arms	Shield	See Pl. 44
9	Monster ? or horse?	Square	
10	Double eagle	Square	Pierpont Morgan catalogue, 1907, vol. III, p. 162.

As regards No. 1, the fleur-de-lis, 'free' is Mr E. P. Goldschmidt's term for a tool not enclosed in some geometrical form.

No. 9 is found only, so far as I know, on the binding of *The Myrrour of the World,* Second Edition, belonging to the Baptist College, Bristol. It is used alone as a diaper on one cover; on the other is a diaper of No. 6. A rather similar circular stamp was used at Oxford (Gibson, op. cit. stamp No. 31).

[2] The list is given in the Remarks on Pl. IX of *Bindings in Cambridge Libraries.*

[3] See my remarks in *Thirty Bindings,* Pl. I; to the examples of this stamp-type quoted there should be added those reproduced by Messrs Hulshof and Schretlen, *De Kunst der oude Boekbinders,* Utrecht, 1921, Pl. V, No. 30 and Pl. VII, No. 17; cf. also the panel of Peter Actors (E. P. Goldschmidt, op. cit. Pl. XLI).

[4] Gibson, op. cit. stamp 30.

[5] This stamp passed later to the binder who worked for Henry Jacobi: Weale, p. xxxv, and R. 102.

to Europe in the early Middle Ages, and was often used by the artists[1] of the 12th century, from whom it descended to the late medieval stamp cutters.

But another derivation of the stamp is also possible; the crane may be a degenerate descendant of the jaculus[2], a dragon so-called because it darts with the swiftness of a javelin from its home in a tree on to the back of its prey. It is shown, having pounced on its victim, in a Bestiary at the British Museum, and in a carved stone Romanesque ornament at St Margaret's[3], Walmgate, York; and the resemblance between the drawing and the sculpture on the one hand, and our binding stamp on the other, is very striking. But whatever the origin of the stamp, its designer must have been both ignorant and careless to have transformed the fierce hawk or the fiery dragon into the timid and ineffectual crane.

We have now to go from London to Cambridge, where there were at least two craftsmen[4] producing stamped bindings in the 15th century. The connection between them must have been very close; their patterns and several of their stamps are very similar, particularly a dromedary and a lozenge-shaped foliage stamp, and they share two unusual characteristics: each of them generally draws a vertical line or lines down the backs of his books, and each of them places a small tool where the bands of the back come on to the boards. The less known and less important of the two I propose to call the Demon binder, because he owned a stamp representing a small upright Demon[5], with horns and hoofs, which unfortunately is not shown on Pl. 46. I have traced nine bindings by this craftsman, who was at work as late as 1497; that his home was at Cambridge seems certain from three facts:

1. Eight out of the nine bindings are in Cambridge libraries.
2. Of these eight bindings, two cover registers of Pembroke College; these would no doubt be bought as blank note books, already bound, from a Cambridge bookseller, and though they may have been imported by him from London or the Continent, the probability that they are local work is peculiarly strong.
3. One of the stamps on the binding illustrated (Pl. 46) passed into the possession of the well-known Cambridge stationer Nicholas Spierinck, and is found, somewhat worn, on many of the bindings decorated with his signed rolls.

Though none of these facts is conclusive in itself, I venture to think that, taken together, they are decisive, and that we need have no hesitation in definitely claiming this binder for Cambridge.

This being so, it becomes probable that his fellow-binder also worked at Cambridge, and this probability becomes practically a certainty when the evidence is examined. Out of the forty-four known works of this binder seventeen are in old Cambridge libraries; one of them covers another register of Pembroke College; and any remaining doubts are dissipated by a binding at Gonville and Caius College, covering a *Sarum Manual* printed at Paris in 1496 or 1497. It contains an inscription stating that it was

1 E. Mâle, *L'Art religieux du XIIe siècle en France*, Paris, 1924, p. 358, fig. 210.

2 See the article by Mr G. C. Druce on 'The Amphisbaena and its connexions' in *The Archaeological Journal*, Vol. LXVIII, 1910, p. 286.

3 Reproduced in *The Reliquary*, Vol. II, New Series, 1888, Pl. II.

4 See for these two binders *Bindings in Cambridge Libraries*, Pls. XIII and XIV.

5 A reproduction will be found in *Bindings in Cambridge Libraries*, Pl. XV, stamp No. 42.

given to the College by Humphrey de la Pole, son of the Duke of Suffolk, in 1498; books at this time generally travelled unbound[1], and it is almost certain that the binding was executed at Cambridge, for it is hardly possible that, if the donor had it bound at London or elsewhere, he would have hit on a binder also patronized by a Cambridge bookseller.

I propose to call this binder the Unicorn[2] binder, after a type of stamp of which he possessed two variants; judging by surviving examples, he must have been one of the most prolific of our 15th-century binders, and he seems to have been in business for at least twenty years. His work falls into three distinct phases: the first, which probably lasted from about 1485 to 1488, is well represented by a specimen in Jesus College Library (Pl. 47); the stamps are not very thickly massed and no foliage stamps are used; the earlier of the two unicorn stamps is found on these bindings.

The characteristic foliage stamps, and the second unicorn, appear in the next phase (Pl. 48), which lasted from about 1488 till after 1500, and was certainly the most productive period of the bindery. Many of the stamps are excellently cut and were probably imported from Flanders or Brabant, since they closely resemble stamps used there; very likely the binder himself was a foreigner. In the third phase, which lasted for a few years after 1500, most of the earlier stamps, except the unicorn and the dromedary, disappear, and are replaced by a large stamp like a pineapple[3] (Pl. 49), of a type much used in the Low Countries and in England at the beginning of the 16th century.

Besides the Demon and the Unicorn binders, no other 15th-century binders can be definitely placed at Cambridge; but another craftsman, whose bindings[4] often bear a shield-shaped stamp with a monogram, may have worked here, since down one at least of his backs he drew vertical lines as they did; further, out of fifty-three known bindings by him, twenty-two are in old Cambridge libraries; and he owned a lozenge-shaped foliage stamp which was clearly supplied by the same stamp cutter as the stamps of the same type used by the two Cambridge binders. But the evidence is not conclusive, and there are some arguments in favour of London, though none, so far as I know, for any other town. Unfortunately, we know very little about this firm, common as the bindings are; even the order of the initials is uncertain, Weale reading them as G.W., Duff as W.G. on the analogy of a trade mark used by the printer William Gryffyth; but the analogy is not very close and initials seem to have been very arbitrarily placed on the trade marks of the period, so that the correct order of the two letters is uncertain. Both authorities agree in thinking that the monogram represents a binder; but it seems to me probable that the owner was a bookseller who frequently employed the same binder and had his mark put on the bindings executed for him. He probably started in business soon after 1490, and about 1510 he took into partnership I.G., whose initials also appear on the roll illustrated. I reproduce the only binding known to me which has both the stamp and the roll, nor do I know of another instance of the use of the double-headed eagle (Pl. 51); it covers a book in the Library of New College, Oxford, which was printed in 1499, but was probably bound several

[1] Mr E. P. Goldschmidt was the first to stress the importance of this practice for the student of bindings; op. cit. pp. 36 et seq.

[2] There is some ground for thinking that this binder may be Walter Hatley, 'stationarius' to the University, whose business life coincides exactly with the period of this bindery.

[3] On this type of stamp see the remarks on Pl. XIV (p. 42, n. 2) of *Bindings in Cambridge Libraries*.

[4] These bindings are discussed in *Bindings in Cambridge Libraries*, Pl. XV, stamps 33–7.

years later, since rolls do not seem to have been used in England before about 1510[1]. In 1520 the partners acquired a very similar roll bearing that date[2], which appears to be the earliest dated roll known in any country. The latest book in any of these bindings, in the Library of Gonville and Caius College, is dated 1533, which gives the business a life of about forty years.

Cambridge has claims on yet another binder[3], who used a rebus with a hare, a pair of spectacles and the letters H.R., the significance of which I cannot determine.

Two of the only five known bindings by him have been in Cambridge since the early 16th century, and he used a round stamp of a pelican or phoenix, which is clearly by the same engraver and taken from the same drawing as the similar stamp[4] used by the Unicorn binder shown on Pl. 48. But he also owned a nosegay very similar to those used by London binders, and our information about him generally is too

[1] Rolls were used in Germany before 1500 by Johann Rychenbach and at least one other binder. K. Haebler, *Rollen- und Plattenstempel des XVI Jahrhunderts*, Leipzig, 1928, pp. 1 and 377.

[2] K. Haebler, *Der Rollstempel und seine Initialen*, 1924, p. 31, says that we first meet with dated rolls in the fifteen twenties, and that they become commoner from 1526 onwards.

[3] All the known bindings by the 'Rebus binder' are large and none is in very good condition; having failed to get a satisfactory photograph, I reproduce all the stamps known to me used by this binder. The bindings by him are the following:

	DATE AND PLACE OF ISSUE		OWNERSHIP	PRESS-MARK
I	1488	Pavia	Hereford Cathedral Library	E. 2. 10
II	Do.	Do.	Do.	E. 5. 5
III	1489	Venice	Peterhouse	O. 6. 15
IV	Do.	Do.	St Catharine's College	Inc. 16
V	1492	Basle	Lincoln Cathedral Library	Inc. 80

No. V has been rebound; the binding is known to me through an early rubbing belonging to Col. Moss. The stamps are arranged on these bindings in lozenge-shaped compartments, very much as on the other English bindings of the late 15th century. The border is sometimes composed of lines, sometimes of stamp No. 6.

[4] Both stamps closely resemble one used by a Suabian binder who worked for Hildebrand Brandenburg c. 1475 (E. P. Goldschmidt, Pl. V).

scanty to make it possible to localize him; he was probably working for a short time at the very end of the 15th century, since the books bound by him were all printed between 1488 and 1492.

It is equally difficult to place the binder who used a fine lozenge-shaped dragon which he always placed sideways as on the cover reproduced; indeed, on most of his bindings[1] he used no other ornaments and he seems to have possessed no more than two stamps in all, which are both shown on Pl. 52; this binder was certainly working as late as 1505.

Another binder, working about 1500, used a triangular stamp of a greyhound, and a roundel representing the martyrdom of St Sebastian (Pl. 53); the latter stamp has no fellows, so far as I know, on English bindings, but it recalls a series of stamps of the Passion[2] of Christ used by an Osnabrück binder who signs with the letter W. The English stamp, however, is more coarsely cut and, like all this binder's tools, seems to be of English manufacture. He may have been a Londoner, since a manuscript bound by him belonged in 1537 to a London Carthusian. I know two examples[3] only of his work, one in Worcester Cathedral Library, the other at Pembroke College.

The last and not the least interesting of these bindings decorated with small stamps just at the beginning of the 16th century is in Westminster Abbey Library (Pl. 54). It covers a book printed in 1495, but as it is lined with leaves from a book printed by Pynson in 1502 it cannot be 15th-century work. Three of the stamps on it—the large round dragon, the lobe-shaped dragon, and the two birds addorsed—are from Romanesque models; all three types were used in England in the 12th century[4], and it is probable that these stamps are survivals from that period; they look too well cut to be English 15th-century work, and they are not likely to have been imported since there is no foreign counterpart of the round dragon, though the two other types are found on German 15th-century bindings. The border of this binding is interesting, and the stamps of which it is composed are of a rare type; the only similar border known to me occurs on the binding of an 11th or 12th-century Bulgarian Psalter[5] in the Public

[1] The list of the bindings is as follows:

	DATE AND PLACE OF ISSUE		OWNERSHIP	PRESSMARK AND REFERENCE
I	1486	n.p.	University College, Oxford	G. 84. 11
II	1490	Strassburg	Pembroke College	C. 5 (Minns 8)
III	1492	Basle	St Paul's Cathedral	22. D. 14
IV	1497	Paris	Gonville and Caius College	F. 16. 18 (Schneider 85)
V	1497	Venice	Lincoln Cathedral	Inc. 44 (see Pl. 52)
VI	1497	Venice	Bodley's Library	Ash. 572
VII	1500	Paris	Do.	Auct. 2. Q. 3. 15
VIII	1504	London	Shrewsbury School	E. V. 26
IX	1505	Paris	Do.	B. IV. 10
X	c. 1505–15	n.p.	Unknown	Sold at Sotheby's, 29 June 1927, Lot 54

On No. II see *Bindings in Cambridge Libraries*, Pl. XV, stamps 15–17.

[2] See *Bindings in Cambridge Libraries*, Pl. XV, stamps 1–10.

[3] See *Bindings in Cambridge Libraries*, Pl. XV, stamps 47 and 48.

[4] Weale, R. 39. On this binding see my contribution to *Jahrbuch der Einbandkunst*, Vol. II; of the stamp-types mentioned, the round dragon is found on Winchester bindings (see Pl. 4); the lobe-shaped dragon in practically all the Romanesque groups; for the two birds see Appendix E, stamp 38. The German 15th-century variant, which was used by the Carthusians at Wedderen near Dülmen in Westphalia, is reproduced by Mr E. P. Goldschmidt, Pl. CVII.

[5] See Pavel Simoni, *An attempt at a collection of information as to the History and Technique of the Bookbinding Art in Russia*, Society of Lovers of Ancient Literature, 1903, Pl. III, fig. 5. Dr Minns, who translated the title for me, says that the author gives no information on the date of the binding.

Library of Leningrad. The two birds are originally Persian[1], and the little plant between them represents the sacred tree HOM, which stands at the doors of Paradise, and heals with its sap all maladies of body and soul; this motive came to the West in the ornament of early woven silks, of which many fine specimens survive in European museums.

There were certainly other craftsmen[2] producing stamped bindings in England before 1500, but they do not seem to have been of great interest. Indeed, the whole subject is a little disappointing; the craft was so much in the hands of foreigners that one can do little but chronicle the various foreign influences that appear, mostly independent of one another; there is no continuous development of a national style, nothing indeed which is distinctively English, except perhaps the cut leatherwork of the Scales binder, until in the reign of Henry VIII we reach the large panel stamps with the Royal Arms. These may fairly be claimed as representing English taste, since they are without parallel abroad. But many of them were used by foreigners, and it is quite possible that they were engraved on the Continent for the English market. One of them, on an empty binding in the Westminster Abbey Library (Pl. 55), has been claimed for the reign of Edward IV, on the ground that the supporters are the white lions of the Earldom of March. But the Royal Arms, with these supporters, are found in a manuscript which is dated 1500[3]; the small stamps found on the binding seem to be of the 16th century rather than the 15th, and the panel itself is far too close to the other heraldic panels to be much earlier than they. A similar panel occurs on a book dated 1522, which is now in the Prussian State Library[4]; and both panels were probably engraved not many years before then.

[1] Or even Sumerian; animals affrontés, separated by a tree, are to be seen on a games board dug up at Ur in the season 1927–8, and reproduced in *The Illustrated London News*, March 3rd, 1928; it belongs now to the Baghdad Museum. These two birds are much more like the patterns of woven silks than the lobe-shaped stamp of two mysterious monsters used by the 12th-century London binder (see Pls. 6 and 8); see for instance the reproductions given in Mr A. F. Kendrick's *Catalogue of Early Medieval Woven Fabrics in the Victoria and Albert Museum*, 1925, Pls. XI and XIV.

[2] See Appendix J.

[3] Royal MS. 16. F. II.

[4] See Mr E. P. Goldschmidt, p. 61, n. 1; he is mistaken in thinking that this panel is the same as that in the Westminster Abbey Library.

APPENDIX A

Early Irish Bindings and Satchels

VERY LITTLE ATTENTION HAS BEEN PAID BY STUDENTS OF binding to these works; and I deeply regret that I did not realize their importance in time to make a serious examination of them. All the four following examples[1] have been excellently reproduced and briefly described in a paper contributed by Mr J. J. Buckley to the *Journal of the Royal Society of Antiquaries of Ireland* (Series VI, Vol. V), Vol. XLV, Pt IV, December 31st, 1915, pp. 300 et seq.

(1) Satchel in Trinity College, Dublin, traditionally associated with the Book of Armagh, though not really made for it: see Pls. 2 and 3.

(2) Satchel in the National Museum, Dublin, traditionally associated with the shrine called the Breac Moédoig, but probably not made for it.

(3) Satchel at Corpus Christi College, Oxford, probably made for the ancient Irish missal which it now contains.

(4) Bookbinding at the Franciscan Friary, Merchants' Quay, Dublin, on a 17th-century life of St Columba, written on vellum. The Librarian, Father Gregory Cleary, O.F.M., tells me that the manuscript has been adapted to the binding, which is of much earlier date and was no doubt selected by the pious scribe or his patron as an appropriate cover for the biography of the ancient saint.

I am personally quite unqualified to give an opinion regarding the date of these four very interesting productions, which I have not even seen. Irish antiquaries preserve a discreet silence on the subject; but a recent event supports my nebulous feeling that the satchels and binding may belong to the 11th century. This is the publication by Sir Israel Gollancz of a drawing in the margin of p. 225 of the Anglo-Saxon MS. known as the Caedmon

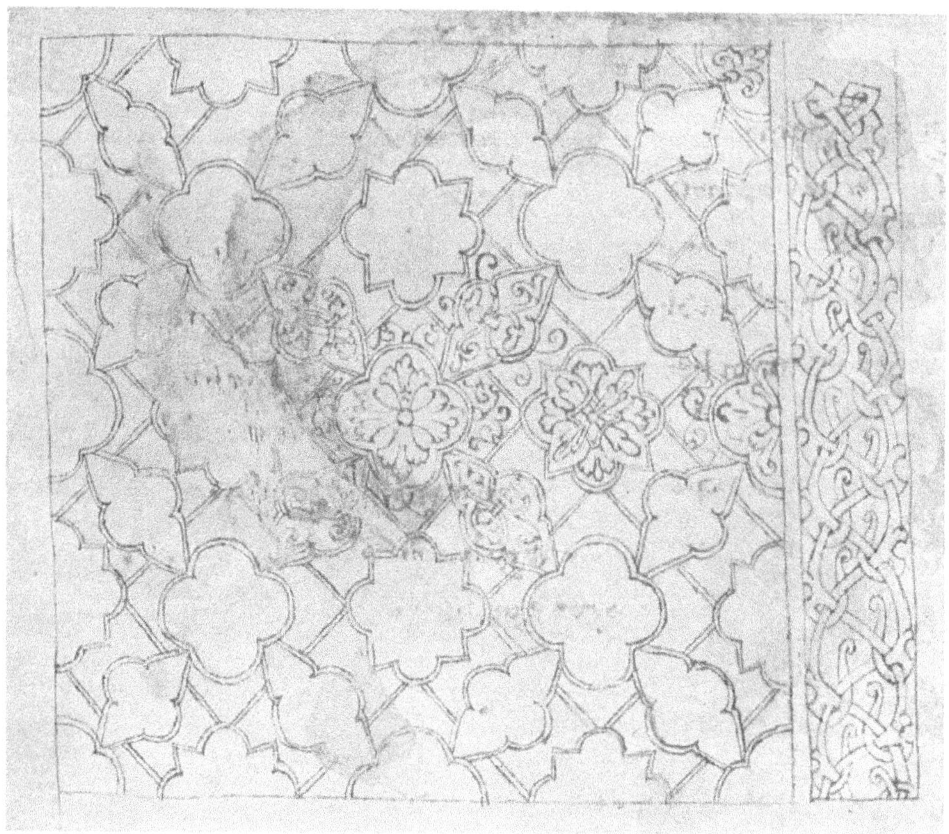

[1] Dr R. A. S. Macalister in *The Archaeology of Ireland*, 1928, p. 319, says that No. 1 of my list "looks like a conscious piece of archaizing", and that the interlacements on No. 2 "prove upon analysis to be rather trivial

Manuscript which is now in Bodley's Library, Oxford (Junius XI). Sir Israel suggests that this is a design for the binding of the book; but Mr Strickland Gibson[1] pointed out that the lavishly decorated[2] back and the absence of bands made this improbable and that it is much more likely to be a design for a book satchel; and for exactly the same reasons I had come to exactly the same conclusion before seeing his article. The likeness between the drawing and the Book of Armagh satchel is obvious; and the former is perhaps even closer to Nos. 2 and 4 of my list. The Caedmon MS. is placed by experts about A.D. 1000; the drawing in it is presumably nearly contemporary; and this is my only real reason for assigning the Irish leatherwork to the 11th century.

It is not easy to see how the ornament of these objects was produced; small metal stamps, large panels, the knife and the graver all seem equally impossible. I am fortunate in being able to quote the explanation proposed by Mr Alfred de Burgh, sub-Librarian of Trinity College, Dublin, who has made a special study of the 'Book of Armagh' satchel:

> "I think that the piece of cowhide was well soaked[3] in water, probably after the lines of the pattern had been traced on it with a pointed or flat bone. Hard wooden or bone implements of various widths were used to press down the background, leaving the higher parts in relief. I have always thought that part of the pressure was applied on the back of the leather...."

Mr de Burgh adds that a friend of his decorated several bindings in intricate interlaced patterns by this method, and that the leather retained the pattern when dry.

* * * * * * * *

The three bindings at Fulda cover the manuscripts entitled the Victor Codex and the Ragyndrudis Codex, and a book of the Gospels, all dating from the 9th century or earlier. The reproductions of all three bindings are unfortunately most unsatisfactory, and I am unable even to distinguish the ornamentation of the first binding. The second has a number of small pieces cut out of the leather, forming a pattern, being thus decorated on the same principle as some early Coptic[4] bindings and some vellum[5] bindings of the early 17th century. The third has an incised saltire within a rectangular frame; in each of the four triangular compartments thus formed is a triquetra of one band, drawn with the knife or graver. This ornament at once suggests a connection with Celtic art, as an exactly similar triquetra is found on a slab at Clonmacnois[6] and on three pre-Scandinavian crosses in the Isle of Man[7].

This relationship recognized, it becomes significant that the manuscript of the Gospels was written and signed by Cadmug, an Irishman, and that the Victor Codex has glosses in an Irish hand. The Ragyndrudis Codex, on the other hand, seems to have no connection with Ireland; but according to an ancient tradition, which is accepted by modern German scholars, it belonged to the Anglo-Saxon Saint Boniface, the Apostle of the Frisians, and was injured

combinations of circles and other curves, such as would scarcely satisfy an artist of the best period of the style". Unfortunately, the learned author does not enlighten us further and gives us no clue as to the archaizing period which may have produced these objects.

1 In the *Bodleian Quarterly Record*, Vol. V, No. 54 (Aug. 23rd, 1927). The facsimile of the drawing is in the reproduction of the Caedmon MS. published for the British Academy, 1927.

2 The design for the back is curiously like some of the backs of Parisian mid-16th century bindings, e.g. *Maioli, Canevari and others*, Pl. 42.

3 Not boiled as the name 'cuir bouilli' suggests; my friend, Mr Paul Hardy, who has made the experiment, tells me that boiling renders leather as brittle as glass and quite impossible to work.

4 See the article by Herr Paul Adam, in *Festschrift Loubier*, 1923, pp. 163–5.

5 See *Thirty Bindings*, Pl. XVII.

6 H. S. Crawford, *Handbook of carved ornament from Irish Monuments of the Christian period*, p. 45 and fig. 9, M.

7 P. M. C. Kermode, *Manx Crosses*, Derby, 1907, p. 35; a list of triquetras in the British Isles is given by J. Romilly Allen, *The Early Christian Monuments of Scotland*, Edinburgh, 1903, Pt I, p. 304, but I do not know how many of the examples he quotes are of the simple form found on this binding. I do not claim that the ornament was confined to the British Isles; it may be seen, for example, in the 9th-century chancel of Sta Maria-degli-Angeli, Assisi; reproduced by R. de Lasteyrie, *L'architecture religieuse en France à l'époque romane*, Paris, 1912, fig. 196.

when he and his companions were massacred in A.D. 755[1]. All three manuscripts therefore are connected with the British Isles, and since the only other early European decorated leatherwork is either English or Irish, it is at least possible that the British Isles should have the credit for the three Fulda bindings also. But, whatever the date and origin of these may be, they seem from the reproductions to be greatly inferior to the specimens at Dublin and Stonyhurst.

[1] I take my particulars of the Fulda manuscripts from an article by Dr Carl Scherer, 'Die Codices Bonifatiani', in *Festgabe zum Bonifatius-Jubiläum,* Fulda, 1905.

APPENDIX B

List, Classification and Early Ownership of the Romanesque Bindings

	TITLE	DATE	OWNERSHIP	PRESSMARK	REFERENCE	REPRODUCTION
I	Salomonis Liber Sapientiae	Early 13th cent.	London, British Museum	MS. 24076	Weale, R. 2 & 3; Weale & Taylor, No. 2	Fletcher, *Bindings*, p. 8 (β); Fletcher, *English*, I (β); Haseloff, p. 517 (α & β)[1]
II	Psalterium glossatum	Early 13th[2] cent.	Do.	MS. 10924	Weale, R. 4 & 5; Weale & Taylor, No. 4	Unpublished
III	Ivo Carnotensis Epistolae	12th cent.	Montpellier, Library of the Faculty of Medicine	MS. 231	Weale, R. 6 & 7	Birkenmajer, Pls. XX & XXI (α & β)
IV	Mattheus glossatus	12th cent.	Montpellier (as above)	MS. 155	Weale, R. 8 & 9	Haseloff, p. 522 (α & β); Birkenmajer, Pls. XVIII & XIX (α&β)
V	Liber de terris regis in Winton	c. 1148	London, Soc. of Antiquaries	—	Weale, R. 10 & 11	Burlington, Pl. II (β), *Victoria County History of Hampshire*, Vol. I, Pls. facing pp. 528 & 530 (α & β); *English Binding before* 1500, Pls. 4 & 5 (α & β)
VI–IX	Bible (Latin), 4 vols.	Late 12th cent.	Durham, Cathedral Library	A. II. 1	Weale, R. 12–19	Pl. 9 (VII α)
X	? Boethius de Trinitate[3]	—	? Paris, Bibliothèque Mazarine	—	Weale, R. 20 & 21; Weale & Taylor, No. 4	Pls. 24 & 25 (α & β)
XI	Dionysius de Coelesti Hierarchia, etc.	12th cent.	Hereford, Cathedral Library	—	Weale, R. 22 & 23	Pls. 20 & 21 (α & β)
XII	Ysaias glossatus	12th cent.	Durham, Cathedral Library	A. III. 17	Weale, R. 24 & 25	Burlington, Pl. III (α): V. & A. Museum, Photographs 49682 & 49683 (α & β)
XIII	Leviticus-Numeri glossati	12th cent.	Do.	A. III. 2	Weale, R. 26 & 27	Burlington, Pl. IV (α): V. & A. Museum, Photographs 49684 & 49685; Pls. 21 *a* & 21 *b* (α & β)
XIV	Psalterium glossatum	12th cent.	Do.	A. III. 7	Weale, R. 28 & 29	Pls. 22 & 23 (α & β)
XV	Evangelia glossata	—	Paris, Bibliothèque Ste-Geneviève	39 Bc. 9	Weale, R. 30 & 31	Unpublished
XVI	Summa super Gratiani decretum	Early 13th cent.	London, British Museum	MS. 24659	Weale, R. 32 & 33; Weale & Taylor, No. 5	Pls. 10 & 11 (α & β)
XVII	Inquisitio de terrarum donatoribus	1185	London, Record Office	—	Weale, R. 34 & 35	Pls. 6 & 7 (α & β)

[1] α and β denote the upper and lower covers respectively.

[2] The dates assigned to this and the other MSS. in the British Museum are given on the authority of Mr E. G. Millar. The handwriting of this manuscript suggests an English origin.

[3] The title, ownership and even the present existence of this manuscript are doubtful; no title is given by Weale in his earlier work, and the manuscript is not now discoverable in the Mazarine Library, in spite of repeated research. It had seemed to me possible that Weale mistook the name of the Library in his earlier work, and the title of the manuscript later; but a personal investigation at the Mazarine Library makes me fear that the binding was there and has now been destroyed. For in the catalogue of MSS. (printed 1885) a MS. of Boethius de Trinitate described as 13th century is stated to be in "Reliure ancienne: plats en carton couverts de cuir gaufré", which might mean such a binding as that shown on Pls. 24 and 25. The MS. has now been rebound: it is very much the same in workmanship and character as most of the other MSS. in these bindings, having a neat rivulet of text meandering through a forest of commentary.

APPENDIX B

	TITLE	DATE	OWNERSHIP	PRESSMARK	REFERENCE	REPRODUCTION
XVIII	Petrus Comestor, Historia Evangelica	13th cent.	London, British Museum	Egerton MS. 272	Weale, R. 36 & 37; Weale & Taylor, No. 6	Brassington, *History*, Pl. 8 (β); Fletcher, *English*, II (β)
XIX	Constantinus Africanus[1]	Late 12th cent.	Do.	Egerton MS. 2900	Weale & Taylor, Introduction, p. iv	Pls. 29 & 30 (α & β)
XX	Evangelium secundum Lucam	Late 12th cent	Do.	Add. MS. 35167	Weale & Taylor, No. 1	Haseloff, p. 519; Birkenmajer, Pls. XXII & XXIII (α & β)
XXI	Cartulary of St Swithin's, Winchester[2]	1130–50	Do.	Add. MS. 15350	Weale & Taylor, No. 3	Unpublished
XXII	Hegesippus, Historia de Excidio Judaeorum	c. 1150	Malvern; C. W. Dyson Perrins, Esq.	—	Weale & Taylor, No. 4	H. Yates Thompson, *Illustrations of 100 MSS.*, Vol. IV, Pls. I & II (α & β)
XXIII	Ezechiel glossatus	Late 12th cent.	Cambridge, Pembroke College	MS. 147	Weale, R. 22; Weale & Taylor, No. 4	M.R.J. (β); see Pls. 26 & 27
XXIV	Petrus Lombardus, Sententiarum libri quatuor	12th cent.	Oxford, Bodley's Library	MS. Rawl. c. 163	Gibson, *Bodley*, 1	Gibson, *Bodley*, Pls. 1 & 2 (α & β); Pl. 8 (β)
XXV	Psalterium glossatum	Late 12th[3] cent.	Prague, Cathedral Library	MS. 47 (Sign A. 133)	Podlaha, 135 et seq.; Haseloff, 513 et seq.	Podlaha, figs. 143 & 144; Haseloff, 514 (α & β)
XXVI	Epistolae Pauli ad Romanos glossatae	Late 12th cent.	Vienna, Staatsbibliothek	MS. 1273	Gottlieb, *Einleitung*, cols. 45–46	Gottlieb, Pls. XXIX & XXX (α & β)
XXVII	Evangelium Marci glossatum	12th cent.	Do.	MS. 1274	Gottlieb, *Einleitung*, cols. 46–7	Gottlieb, Pls. XXXI & XXXII (α & β)
XXVIII	Evangelium Johannis glossatum	—	Vich, Museo Episcopal	—	J. Gudiol, in *Museum*, Barcelona, No. 7, 1913, 241 et seq.	*Museum*, ut cit. p. 243 & plate facing p. 244 (α & β)
XXIX	Evangelium Marci glossatum	—	Halberstadt, Domgymnasium	MS. 48	Haseloff, 508 et seq.	Haseloff, 509 (α & β)
XXX	Evangelium Marci glossatum	Early 12th cent.	Cracow, Jagellon Library	MS. 2470	Birkenmajer, passim	P. Adam in *Archiv für Buchbinderei*, XVII, 1918–19, pp. 43–4; Birkenmajer, Pls. XXIV & XXV (α & β)
XXXI	Evangelium Matthei glossatum	Late 13th cent.	Basle, Universitäts-Bibliothek	B. II. 6	Gottlieb in *Belvedere*, Jan. 1926, p. 22	*Belvedere*, ut cit. Pls. 4 & 5 (α & β)
XXXII	Proverbia Salomonis glossata	—	Lambach	MS. Vellum LXXXVII	Gottlieb in *Belvedere*, ut cit.	*Belvedere*, ut cit. Pls. 1 & 2 (α & β)
XXXIII	Evangelium Marci glossatum	—	Plotzk, Cathedral Library	MS. 143	Birkenmajer in *Jahrbuch der Einbandkunst*, I, 1927, pp. 13 et seq.	*Jahrbuch*, ut cit. Pls. 1 & 2 (α & β)
XXXIV	Paulus glossatus[4]	—	Leipzig, Universitäts-Bibliothek	MS. 91	Husung in *Zeitschrift für Bucherfreunde*, 1927, NF. pp. 19, 28 et seq.	*Zeitschrift*, ut cit. Pls. 29 & 30 (α)
XXXV	Claudianus, Opera[5]	Reign of Henry III, 1216–72	London, British Museum	Add. MS. 6042	Dibdin, *Bibliographical Decameron*, II, 464–5	Dibdin, ut cit. (five stamps only)
XXXVI	Leviticus glossatus	Early 13th cent.	Admont (Styria) Benedictine Monastery	MS. 347	Briefly referred to, with the three following MSS. by Dr P. Buberl, *Die Illuminierten HSS. in Steiermark*, Leipzig, 1911, p. 158	Pl. 16 (α & β)

[1] Has some 13th-century additions, the main portion perhaps written in England; formerly Phillipps MS. 6925; sold at Sotheby's 1903, Lot 287; afterwards Dunn 451: Cf. *Catalogue of additions to the Western MSS. in the British Museum*, 1911–5, p. 413.

[2] This binding is in very poor condition; it would be impossible to reproduce it satisfactorily; six of the stamps are reproduced in Weale and Taylor, Pl. I, 10–15.

[3] So dated by Haseloff, p. 525.

[4] About five-sixths of one cover alone remains.

[5] This binding no longer exists; the MS. was identified for me by Mr J. A. Herbert.

	TITLE	DATE	OWNERSHIP	PRESSMARK	REFERENCE	REPRODUCTION
XXXVII	Apocalypsis glossata	—	Admont	MS. 418	Buberl, ut cit.	Unpublished
XXXVIII	Canonicae epistolae glossatae	—	Do.	MS. 537	Do.	Pl. 28 (α & β)
XXXIX	Evangelium Johannis glossatum	—	Do.	MS. 568	Do.	Unpublished
XL	Evangelium Johannis glossatum	12th cent.	Troyes, Bibliothèque de la Ville	MS. 1023 bis	*Catalogue général des MSS. des Bibliothèques publiques des Départements*, Vol. II	Pls. 14 & 15 (α & β)
XLI	Proverbia, Ecclesiastes, Canticum Canticorum glossata	12th cent.	Do.	MS. 1378	Do.	Pl. 17 (α)
XLII	Evangelium Marci glossatum	12th cent.	Do.	MS. 871	Do.	Pls. 12 & 13 (α & β)
XLIII	Bernardus, de consideratione Excerpta; etc.	12th cent.	Do.	MS. 1838	Do.	Pls. 18 & 19 (α & β)
XLIV	Breviarium	—	Halberstadt, Domgymnasium	MS. 153	*Jahrbuch*, p. 20	*Jahrbuch*, Pls. 3 & 5 (α & β)
XLV	Evangelium Matthei glossatum	12th cent.	Leipzig, Universitäts-Bibliothek	MS. 78	Dr O. Glauning, in *Archiv für Buchgewerbe*, Vol. LXV, 1928, pp. 101–3	*Archiv für Buchgewerbe*, ut cit. Tafel 1 (α) & Tafel 4, stamps 1–6
XLVI	Sacrificiorum mystica interpretatio	—	Admont	MS. 413	None	Unpublished
XLVII	Trenorum glossatus	—	Do.	MS. 415	Do.	Do.

Nos. I–XLV may be classified as follows:—I am unable to classify Nos. XLVI and XLVII, knowing nothing of them except that they exist:

I. English.

- A. Winchester V, XXI, XXII =3
- B. London XVII, XVIII and XXIV =3
- C. Durham VI to IX =4 } =12
- D. ? Oxford XVI =1
- E. ? Canterbury XXXV =1

II. French.

- F. Clairvaux[1] (α) IV, XX, XXX, XLII =4
- G. Clairvaux (β) III, XXXIV and XL =3 } =14
- H. Central European section XXV, XXIX, XXXVI and XXXIX =4
- K. Clairvaux (γ) (different binders) I, XLI and XLIII =3

III. French or English.

(α) *The great stamp cutter section*

- L. Vich section XI, XII, XIII, XXVIII and XXXII =5
- M. Ezechiel section X, XIV, XV, XXIII and XXXIII =5 } =14
- N. Admont section XXXVII and XXXVIII =2
- O. Vienna binding and another (different binders) II and XXVII =2

(β) *Various*

- P. All different binders XIX, XXVI and XXXI =3

IV. German (different binders).

- Q. XLIV and XLV =2

[1] The names of all the classes from F onwards are given merely for convenience of reference.

The number of binders therefore is

A–H, one each = 8, K = 3, L–N, one each = 3; O = 2, P = 3, Q = 2.

Total = 8 + 3 + 3 + 2 + 3 + 2 = 21.

But this total, owing to difficulties of comparison, must be regarded as approximate only.

It will be noticed that more than half the binderies are represented by a single work only; and it is probable that no less have disappeared altogether than survive. We can hardly be wrong in assuming that stamped bindings were produced in the 12th and 13th centuries by at least forty different craftsmen.

OWNERSHIP

A tentative list of the earliest owners of Romanesque bindings, with their approximate dates: I have recorded only the first known possessor of each volume, and none later than 1700. Messrs J. A. Herbert and E. G. Millar have told me about the ownership of some of the volumes in the British Museum; all the other owners have, I think, already been published.

A. ENGLISH

Anonymous: 1520—XVI (D).
Cambridge: John Sudbury: † 1434—XXIII (M).
Canterbury: St Augustine's Abbey: 13th century—XXXV (E).
Durham: Hugh de Puiset: † 1195—VI to IX, XII and XIV (C, L and M).
Durham: Robert de Adington: 12th century—XIII (L).
Hereford: Cathedral Library: 12th century—XI (L).
London: Knights Templars: 1185—XVII (B).
London: Church of St Mary Overy, Southwark: 13th century—XVIII (B).
Pembroke: Dr Younge: 1649—XX (F).
Winchester: St Swithin's Priory: 12th century—XXI (A).
Winchester: Dr Young, Dean of: temp. James I—V (A).

In addition, nos. II (O) and XIX (P) may have been wholly or partly written in England.

B. FRENCH

Clairvaux, Abbey of: presented by Archbishop Henry: † 1175—III, IV, XLII (F and G).
Clairvaux, Abbey of: previously belonged to John of Pisa, Canon of Laon—XLI (K).
Clairvaux, Abbey of: method of acquisition unknown—XL (G), XLIII (K).
Melun, Abbey of St Jean du Jard: ? 12th or 13th century—XV (M).
Paris: P. Noblet, bookseller: 1473—XXXI (P).

C. GERMAN AND POLISH

Admont[1], Abbey of: XXXVI–XXXIX (H and N), XLVI and XLVII.
Altzelle in Saxony, Monastery of: XLV (Q).
Basle, bought at: 1436—XXX (F).
Erfurt: St Paul's Monastery: 14th century—II (O).
Hildesheim, Harderadus Canon of: † c. 1179—XXIX (H).
Lambach, Monastery of: XXXII (L).
Pegau, Abbey of: near Merseburg: before 14th century—XXXIV (G).
Plotzk, Preaching Friars: ? 14th century—XXXIII (M).
Vienna, a Monastery of: XXVI (P) and XXVII (O).

In addition, XLIV (Q) was written at Halberstadt.

[1] One of the Admont bindings contains the inscription 'Pignus archipresbyteri de Gavando'; I do not think that this deserves the importance attached to it by Dr Gottlieb—it does not add to the number of these bindings known to have been on the Continent in the Middle Ages.

THE ROMANESQUE BINDINGS

Counting the Durham Bible (Nos. VI to IX) as one book, we have thirteen books in England before 1700, seven in France, and fifteen in central Europe; the early owners of the remainder are unknown to me.

The list and classification of the bindings bring to light two rather unexpected facts:

(1) The products of several binderies—particularly those in the great stamp cutter class—are very widely scattered; L, for instance, is divided between Durham, Hereford, Lambach and Vich; M between Durham, Cambridge, Melun and Plotzk.

(2) On the other hand, several different binderies are represented in the same early libraries: four each at Durham[1] and Clairvaux; two at Admont; two probably at some Viennese monastery.

I have no satisfactory explanation; the first hypothesis that suggests itself is that some at all events of the bindings are the work of wandering craftsmen; but it is difficult to believe either that men could have lived by such a trade in the 12th century, or that they would have burdened themselves with these absurdly large founts of tools. Obviously, however, these objections are not conclusive; and the only alternative, a wide circulation of bound books, is contrary both to the practice of the 15th century, and to the letter of Adam de Marisco quoted in Appendix K. All that can safely be said is that the large number of different founts on the one hand, and the persistence of certain stamp-types on the other hand, suggest that binders were many and stamp cutters few.

[1] Counting the 13th or 14th-century binding reproduced on Pl. 31.

APPENDIX C

A 13th or 14th-Century English Binding

Author, etc. Stephanus, Archiepiscopus Cantuariensis, *Super Ecclesiasticum*, 13th-century MS.

Ownership. Durham Cathedral Library.

Pressmark. A. III. 28.

Size. 343×227 mm.

Description. Very dark brown leather, probably goatskin; rebacked and the original sides pasted down over new leather c. 1840; the outermost ornament all round is modern.

Previous ownership. An inscription, probably[1] of the 14th century, states that it was presented by Brother Godfrey de Kyppier to the Church of St Cuthbert, Durham.

Reference. The stamps are described by Weale, R. 38.

Remarks. The lower cover is reproduced on Pl. 31; the ornament on the upper cover is arranged in a similar pattern, but two different stamps are used which I reproduce.

The second of these, showing a falcon pouncing on a bird, is the reversed variant of a stamp reproduced in Weale and Taylor, Pl. XXIII, No. 3, from a late 15th-century German binding; it is no doubt of Oriental origin (cf. pp. 20–1 for remarks on a similar type of stamp shown on Pl. 45). Of the stamps shown on Pl. 31 the two birds in foliage forming the outer frame resembles a well-known Erfurt type which has often been reproduced[2]. The double eagle recalls the lobe-shaped stamps found in Classes E, H and K (No. XLIII) of the Romanesque bindings (see p. 9, n. 4 and p. 36); the type, which was popular in the 15th century (see Pl. 51: and Weale, R. 374), no doubt entered medieval art from Oriental woven silks (see E. Mâle, *L'art religieux du XIIième siècle en France*, 1924, p. 351). The animal forming the second frame has a certain resemblance to the stamp found by the Duke of Rutland at Belvoir (see p. 5).

The date of this binding is very uncertain. Weale calls it 13th century, but it has little in common with the Romanesque bindings, and it might belong to the 14th century; it seems probable at all events that the binding precedes the presentation inscription.

We may take it then that this is an English—perhaps Durham—binding not later than the 14th century; but how are we to explain the resemblance between its two most remarkable stamps and two late 15th-century German types? It seems to me that there are four, and only four, possible answers to this question:

1. Chance: the stamp cutters may have hit on the same designs independently; this is most improbable, the types are too unusual and the resemblances too close.

2. Import of German stamps into England: most improbable in the 14th century, though common enough in the 15th.

3. Export of English stamps into Germany in the 15th century: more than improbable.

4. German imitation of English originals: and this I believe to be the true explanation, unexpected as it is. It is certain that German stamp cutters copied Romanesque[3] models;

[1] Information from Mr J. Meade Falkner.

[2] E.g. Weale and Taylor, Pl. III, No. 9; in the text the binding is assigned to Cologne, but no reasons for the attribution are given; the variants which were unquestionably used at Erfurt are mostly vesica-shaped (see e.g. Schwenke's article in *Festgabe Haebler*, 1919, Tafel 2, facing p. 130).

[3] See my Essay in *Jahrbuch*, II

it is also known that English manuscripts[1] travelled to Germany in the Middle Ages, and it has recently been shown that English 14th-century painting[2] influenced Rhenish art; so that, on examination, the theory is not unsupported. One small point in its favour is the fact that the German stamp of the pouncing falcon is reversed; this would naturally happen if the engraver of the matrix copied the English stamp directly.

[1] Some of the finest 12th-century manuscripts in the Nationalbibliothek at Vienna are English; see *Zentralblatt für Bibliothekswesen*, April 1928, p. 195.

[2] See the *Burlington Magazine*, April 1928, p. 159—review by M. H. Bernath of a work by Dr R. Freyhan, *Die Illustrationen zum Casseler Willehalm Codex. Ein Beispiel englischen Einflusses in der rheinischen Malerei des XIV Jahrhunderts.*

APPENDIX D

A Romanesque Binding in the Bibliothèque de la Ville, Troyes

No. XLIII of the list: Pls. 18 and 19

Title, etc. Various tracts:

(1) *Incerti excerpta varia.*
(2) *Exceptiones e v libris beati Bernardi de consideratione ad Eugenium Papam.*
(3) *Incerti speculum caritatis.*

Ownership. Bibliothèque de la Ville, Troyes.

Pressmark. MS. 1838.

Size. 200×135 mm.

Material, etc. Brown leather; a portion, 110×68 mm. in size, is a different piece of leather, much darker in colour; remains of bosses at the four corners and centre and of two clasps. There are two layers of deerskin between the stamped leather and the wooden boards.

Previous ownership. The Cistercian Abbey of Clairvaux.

Remarks. Unquestionably one of the most interesting of these bindings, and important on account of the great differences between the fount of tools used on it and those in vogue elsewhere. The principal stamps are the following:

Upper cover, Pl. 18

1. Lobe-shaped, a two-headed bird: variants in Classes E (see p. 6) and H (*Jahrbuch*, Pl. 4, No. 12); another, rectangular, on Pl. 31; cf. p. 34. Probably this stamp comes from Oriental woven silks.

2. Rectangular, a goat with the inscription 'IRCUS': as Mr G. C. Druce points out to me, the inscription shows that this stamp was copied from a Latin Bestiary. No other stamp resembling this, but a running goat in Class C (see Pl. 9).

3. Rectangular, a dragon, possibly a cockatrice. Another quite different cockatrice in Class P (No. XIX, Pl. 29).

4. Rectangular, a kneeling figure holding a cup, behind him a bird. Probably Ganymede, who, as Mr O. M. Dalton informed me, is engraved on a 12th-century bronze bowl found in the Severn and now in the British Museum: see his article in *Archaeologia*, Vol. LXXII, p. 144.

5. Rectangular, a small full length figure, apparently dressed only in a skirt; in the left hand he holds a spear and in the right a horn which he is blowing; in front of him a small tree or shrub. Some observers have seen a resemblance between this rather comic little figure and Babylonian seals. It occurred to me that he might be intended for Roland, who is sometimes shown in Romanesque sculpture blowing his dread horn (Mâle, pp. 264 et seq.); others would call him more prosaically a huntsman! He should be compared with two figures on No. II (Class N; reproduced by Weale and Taylor, Pl. II, No. 1).

6. Rectangular, oblong: a cable pattern; variant in Class H (*Jahrbuch*, Pl. 5, No. 24).

7. Circular, a rosette: a type of stamp of which there are variants in most of the groups.

Lower cover, Pl. 19

8. Rectangular, an indescribable stamp. When I first saw this, I took it to be a reminiscence of an Egyptian seal, the objects like stalks of ripe corn recalling the Egyptian initial *y* (the flower of the reed) and the object beside them the cartouche often found on scarabs. But no scarabs have their decoration arranged in this fashion; and Mr G. C. Druce suggested that the

stamp was adapted from a drawing found in the early Bestiaries of ant-heaps and cornfields which I reproduce from his photograph of a page in a 10th-century manuscript in the

Royal Library, Brussels (MS. 10074). I had adopted whole-heartedly this delightful suggestion when one day I showed my photograph of the binding to the Duke of Rutland, who at once pointed out the architectural character of the stamp; and on comparing it with the stamp of a church reproduced in *Jahrbuch*, Pl. 4, Nos. 16–18, it became obvious to us both that the Troyes stamp is simply the lower half of the sinister side of the building, without the roof or tower[1]. I have no doubt that this is the true explanation of the stamp, prosaic as it is in comparison with Mr Druce's or even my own.

9. Rectangular, a nude figure standing: this is to be explained in conjunction with No. 11 below.

10. Rectangular, almost wholly effaced: possibly Samson and the lion, for which cf. Appendix E, No. 3.

11. Rectangular, a dog running in front of a tree: clearly the same animal as that shown on the Duke of Rutland's stamp (see p. 5). I believe that this stamp and No. 9 taken together illustrate the legend of the woutre, as shown in a Bestiary at the Bibliothèque de l'Arsenal, Paris (for which see Cahier and Martin, *Mélanges d'Archéologie*, Paris, 1851, Vol. II, Pl. XIX). The woutre was an animal which, when it saw a naked man, passed by on the other side and left him unscathed, but upon a man fully clothed it fell with tooth and claw, and devoured him to the last gaiter button. The woutre represents the evil one, and the naked man those who have renounced the pomps and vanities of this wicked world, against whom Satan is powerless; the clothed man those who love earthly possessions and are the prey of the Devil.

Mr G. C. Druce, unfortunately, will not accept my theory, pointing out that the woutre is a late French corruption of the wivre, a serpent, and that it does not assume the form of

[1] For an equally meaningless use of an architectural stamp, cf. No. XXV of the list on p. 30, which has two rows of repeated impressions of the pinnacle of the church spire, the alternate stamps in the upper row being inverted!

a dog or lion till after 1300. But the two stamps are so exactly like the drawing that I cannot help believing the transformation to be earlier than any of the surviving manuscripts which illustrate it.

12. A dog passant.

In addition, there are three small stamps, a leaf-like ornament, a segment of a circle and a small fleur-de-lis.

I think this binding is more likely to belong to the 13th century than the 12th for the following reasons:

A. The slovenly and ignorant use of the stamps suggests that it comes from a period of monastic decadence—i.e. after 1200.

B. Of the three analogies to the double-headed eagle, the Canterbury variant (see p. 6) was used on a 13th-century manuscript; that shown on Pl. 31 is admittedly 13th century, or later; the third is found in Class H which also includes the horseman with the rowel spur—another feature suggesting the 13th century. The analogies to stamps 6 and 8 also belong to Class H.

C. My explanation of stamps 9 and 11 also points in the same direction.

APPENDIX E

Stamps in Class M of the Romanesque Bindings

The stamps on No. XXIII (Pls. 26 and 27) are as follows:

A. *Figure subjects.*

Nos. 1 and 2. St Peter and St Paul[1]. Variants of one or both, in Classes E, F, G, H, L and P (No. XIX). The joint cultus of St Peter and St Paul was very popular in the 12th century. The great monastery of Cluny was under their protection, so was the abbey of St Augustine's, Canterbury, and no less than sixty-one churches in Kent alone[2]. No other saints are found on these bindings.

No. 3. Samson and the lion. Variants in Classes A, H, L and P (No. XIX). The group is common in 12th-century sculpture[3]; and, like so many other motives of Romanesque ornament, is derived from the decoration of Eastern woven silks of the 6th to the 8th centuries. Several of these, variously assigned to Constantinople, Alexandria and Hither Asia, are preserved in the Victoria and Albert Museum, London[4], the Schlossmuseum, Berlin, the Cathedral Treasury at Coire, and elsewhere. The group has been variously explained; some would see in it merely a reminiscence of some lion-tamer's act in the great Circus at Byzantium; others, Hercules and the Nemean lion; others consider it to be originally Mithraic[5]; others, that it illustrates Psalm lviii, 6, "Break out the great teeth of the young lions, O Lord[6]"; others, finally, suggest David as an alternative to Samson. I am certainly not going to attempt to decide so vexed a question, but two points at all events appear indisputable. First, that Samson is a rather more likely figure than David, who, to illustrate the text (1 Samuel xvii, 34–6) correctly, should be accompanied by a lamb, and is in fact so accompanied on an Irish Cross[7], and on a silver dish discovered at Kyrenia[8], in Cyprus, which is now in the Pierpont Morgan collection[9]. Second, that two 12th-century stamp cutters did take the figure for Samson, since the versions on Bindings XIX and XXXIX are labelled thus.

No. 4. Seated King. Variants in Classes L (No. XI) and N (No. XXXVIII). On the latter binding the King is shown correctly as part of a Jesse tree; the stamp strikingly resembles the Kings in the 12th-century Jesse windows of St-Denis, Chartres and York[10].

No. 5. King riding carrying a sceptre. No variants with the same attributes; but Kings riding carrying palm branches are found in Classes G, K (No. I) and L. No special elucidation of the stamp on our binding seems called for; 12th-century Kings may well have ridden

[1] St Peter is unrecognizable in the rubbing; but his key is discernible on the binding.

[2] Dr G. F. Browne, 'The Cultus of St Peter and St Paul', in *The Importance of Women in Anglo-Saxon Times, and other addresses*, 1919, p. 59.

[3] For reproductions see A. K. Porter, *Romanesque Sculpture of the Pilgrimage Roads*, 10 vols., Boston, 1923, Nos. 18, 46, 68, 166, 180, 338, 925, 948, 1136, 1219, 1342; and the same author's *Lombard Architecture*, I, 395; II, 222, 273, 334, 389; III, 35, 104, 157, 177, 210, 211, 247, 285, 307, 346, 453, 462, 523 and 544. C. E. Keyser, *Norman Tympana and Lintels*, 1927, figs. 84 and 85.

[4] See A. F. Kendrick, *Catalogue of early medieval woven fabrics in the V. and A. Museum, Dept. of Textiles*, 1925, p. 23 and Pl. II, and O. von Falke, *Kunstgeschichte der Seidenweberei*, Berlin, 1913, Vol. I, p. 54, and Abb. 71. Both authors mention and briefly discuss the various interpretations of the group, and give lists of the surviving fabrics decorated with it.

[5] A. K. Porter, *Romanesque Sculpture*, Vol. I, p. 189: he follows F. Cumont, *The Mysteries of Mithra*, 1903, p. 228.

[6] V. Terret, *La Sculpture bourguignonne*, Autun, 1925, Pl. XIV.

[7] H. S. Crawford, *Handbook of carved ornament from Irish monuments of the Christian period*, Dublin, 1926, p. 70, and Pl. XLIII, No. 131.

[8] *Burlington Magazine*, Vol. X, p. 356.

[9] But there is no lamb in the fine initial *B* of the 12th-century Winchester Bible, which shows David killing the lion (*Burlington Fine Arts Club Exhibition of Miniatures*, 1908, Pl. 78); here, however, David is adequately identified, as the initial illustrates the Psalms and in the upper compartment he is shown killing the bear.

[10] E. Mâle, *L'art religieux du XIIième siècle en France*, Paris, 1924, pp. 169, 170; and the Rev. F. Harrison, *The Painted Glass of York*, 1927, pp. 37–8.

sometimes with their royal insignia. If the stamp has a meaning, it may represent Constantine, who is shown not infrequently on horseback in 12th-century sculpture[1]. But the Kings carrying palm branches obviously require explanation—and I am quite unable to explain them, for none of the three interpretations which suggest themselves is quite satisfactory:

A. The palm branch may be a misunderstood sceptre; but this is very unlikely—the obvious is substituted for the obscure—not *vice versa*.

B. The stamp may represent Christ entering Jerusalem, since, on the tympanum[2] of the church at Aston Eyre, and in the 13th-century painted glass[3] at Bourges, He is shown carrying a palm branch; but the absence of a halo seems to negative this explanation decisively.

C. The stamp may represent the Magi who are often shown on horseback in 12th-century art[4], though never, so far as I know, carrying palms. But they are represented kneeling with palms in their hands[5] on the Cathedral at Münster; and they may be seen riding in front of palm trees, both to and from Bethlehem, in the English 12th-century Psalter[6] at Hildesheim. On the whole this seems to me the most likely guess, and the fact that the stamp is never shown thrice repeated does not lead me to abandon it. For very little study reveals that these early binders paid not the smallest heed to the significance of the stamps they used. Jesse sleeps forlorn without his tree (No. XXXVIII); the Kings, his progeny, hang horizontally aligned in mid-air, grasping rootless volatile branches (Nos. XXIII and XI); and, most curious of all, two repetitions of the Holy Dove meet each other in level flight (No. XXXVII).

B. *Grotesques.*

No. 6. Amphisbaena }
No. 7. Two-headed grotesque } Three other two-headed grotesques in Classes L and O (Nos. II and XXVII). The amphisbaena, or two-headed dragon, is common in medieval art[7], but the other grotesques appear to be original inventions of the great stamp cutter of whom I have spoken elsewhere[8].

C. *Animals.*

No. 8. Bird.

No. 9. Bird. Variants on No. XIV (see stamp 39 below) and in Class P (No. XXXI).

No. 10. Dragon. Variants in, I think, all the groups and on almost all the bindings; cf. No. 35 below. This type of stamp was also used in the 15th century[9]; the shape and ornament were perhaps copied originally from 12th-century shields, though as Dr Minns pointed out to me, this is by no means certain, since the dragons on shields are placed the other way up[10].

No. 11. Fishes. No doubt the sign of the Zodiac. Variants on No. XIV (stamp No. 32 below); and in Classes C and L (No. XI). I regret that no clear impression of this stamp is available.

D. *Formal or foliated stamps.*

No. 12. Palmette. A type no less common than the dragon No. 10. This is perhaps the finest example of it; in detail and engraving it closely resembles the six-leaved flower, No. 29 below.

[1] A. K. Porter, *Romanesque Sculpture*, Nos. 763, 774, 924, 1008, 1011, 1052, 1093, 1093 A; Mâle, op. cit. p. 248. Mr Porter doubts whether all the riders represent Constantine and thinks that some may be of Eastern origin; see his Vol. I, p. 188.

[2] C. E. Keyser, op. cit. fig. 90.

[3] J. Romilly Allen, *Early Christian Symbolism in Great Britain and Ireland*, 1887, p. 302, n. 1.

[4] A. K. Porter, *Romanesque Sculpture*, Nos. 102, 140, 144, 191, 234, 773, 806; Mâle, op. cit. p. 68, n. 3.

[5] Hugo Kehrer, *Die Heiligen drei Könige*, Leipzig, 1909, Abb. 168.

[6] Kehrer, op. cit. Abb. 135 and 139.

[7] See the article by Mr G. C. Druce, a great authority on medieval zoology, in the *Archaeological Journal*, Vol. LXV (1910), pp. 285–317.

[8] See pp. 11 and 46.

[9] See my Essay in *Jahrbuch*, II; also post, Pl. 54.

[10] See the shields in the Bayeux Tapestry; Stothard's reproduction, Pls. III and XVI.

No. 13. Foliage stamp. Variant in Class Q (No. XLV).

No. 14. Rosette. A type found in practically all the groups.

No. 15. Small Roundel, cf. No. 22.

No. 16. Scroll or foliage stamp; somewhat akin to stamp 42 below, and to the curved foliage stamp in Class A.

Of the other bindings in the group, No. XXXIII is closest to No. XXIII, since they share no less than eight stamps, namely, Nos. 1, 2, 3, 7, 8, 11, 13 and 16.

No. XXXIII has fourteen stamps in all, the six others being the following:

No. 17. A kneeling Elder. Variants in Classes G and L. Though usually described as a kneeling King, this figure is really one of the Elders described in Revelation iv, 4 and v, 8:

"And round about the Throne were four and twenty seats, and upon the seats I saw four and twenty elders sitting, clothed in white raiment; and they had on their heads crowns of gold....And when He had taken the book, the four beasts and four and twenty elders fell down before the Lamb, having every one of them harps and golden vials full of odours, which are the prayers of saints."

In both variants the smoke of the incense may be clearly seen rising from the vials. These elders are common in 12th-century monumental sculpture,[1] but they disappear about 1200.

No. 18. David with his harp. Variants on No. XIV (see stamp 32); also in Classes B, D, G, H, L, O (No. II) and P (No. XXXI).

No. 19. Running dog. Variant in Class K (No. I).

No. 20. Another—and very inferior—palmette.

No. 21. Another rosette with eight leaves.

No. 22. A small roundel. I cannot be sure whether this is the same as No. 15 above or not.

No. X (Pls. 24 and 25) is close to both bindings, having stamps 1, 2, 10, 12, 13, 17 and 21; also

No. 23.[2] A crowned and robed figure walking to the left, and carrying a palm branch in the left hand. Weale states in his description of No. XIV (*α*) that the figure is "a wise virgin crowned, with a lamp in her right hand, and a palm branch in her left", but very careful examination of No. XIV by Mr J. Meade Falkner, and of facsimiles of Nos. X, XIV and XV by myself, has failed to reveal the lamp. Deprived of this attribute, the figure may be either (1) a royal martyr, or (2) one of the Elect of Revelation vii, 9:

"Clothed with white robes and palms in their hands."

Neither explanation is wholly satisfactory; against the former is the fact that there are no saints but St Peter and St Paul on these bindings [unless the Bishops in Classes K (Nos. I

[1] See Mâle, op. cit. pp. 7, 380, 439–40, and A. K. Porter, *Romanesque Sculpture*, Vol. I, pp. 141–3, and Index.

[2] A discovery which I ought to have made very much earlier than the last moment of the eleventh hour convinces me that this figure does represent one of the Elect of Revelation vii, 9. I was inclined to doubt this on account of the crown, but though in manuscripts the elect are not crowned (see n. 1, p. 42), they appear thus in a 13th-century carving of the Last Judgment at Notre-Dame de Paris, and at other French cathedrals of the same period—Reims, Chartres, Bourges, Amiens and Rouen—angels wait to crown them at the doors of Paradise, in fulfilment of Rev. ii, 10, "Be ye faithful unto death and I will give thee a crown of life" (Mâle, *L'art religieux du XIIIe siècle*, Paris, 1925, p. 387).

This identification makes it probable that several of these stamps were intended to be combined into a representation of the Last Judgment, such as we often find in 12th and 13th century art, namely

1. Christ seated on a rainbow (Rev. iv, 3): see Birkenmajer, Pl. XXVI, 10.

2. The Holy Lamb (Rev. v, 6 and xiv, 1): see stamp 26, p. 42. Christ enthroned and the Holy Lamb are both shown in a window at Bourges (Mâle, *op. cit.* p. 367).

3–6. The evangelical animals (Rev. iv, 6–7): see Birkenmajer, Pl. XXVI, 3, 4, 6–9.

7. The angels with trumpets (Rev. viii, 2): see Pl. 28.

8. The four and twenty Elders: see stamp 17, p. 41.

9. The Elect.

and XLI) and N be saints]; against the latter, the fact that the Elect are not commonly represented as crowned.[1]

No. 24. Two watchers on a tower. Variants in Classes H and L. Similar watchers may be seen on an ivory casket at Stuttgart[2] and it is suggested by Mr A. Goldschmidt that they are watching over the safety of the precious reliquary; this is no doubt the *raison d'être* of our watchers also.

No. 25. The Holy Dove. Variant in Class N, on No. XXXVIII shown at the head of the Jesse tree.

No. 26. The Agnus Dei with cross and banner. Variants in Classes D, E, F, L and N.

No. 27. The winged bull of St Luke. Variants on No. XIV (cf. stamp No. 37 below) and in Classes ? A,[3] F, G and L.

No. 28. Bird passant with palmette tail. Variants in Classes C, H, K (No. XLI β), L.

No. X, therefore, has thirteen stamps in all; No. XV, though a large book, has seven only, namely, Nos. 1, 10, 23, 24 and

No. 29. A beautiful round six-leaved flower;[4] cf. No. 12 above. This stamp is reproduced by Weale (R. 30, p. 99): a very similar eight-leaved flower is found in Class B (reproduced by Weale, R. 34–5, p. 101).

No. 30. A fine oblong conventional acanthus: similar stamps in Classes B and O (No. XXVII).

No. 31. A geometrical tile pattern stamp (reproduced by Weale, R. 30, p. 99).[5]

Finally on No. XIV (Pls. 22 and 23) we find stamps 6, 7, 23, 24, 30 and 31; also

No. 32. Another David; cf. No. 18 above.

No. 33. A mounted Knight.

No. 34. A half-length figure with shield beneath a canopy. Variants in Classes C, H, K (Nos. I and XLI).

No. 35. Another lobe-shaped dragon; cf. No. 10 above.

No. 36. Another pair of fishes; cf. No. 11 above.

No. 37. Another winged bull; cf. No. 27 above.

No. 38. Two birds addorsed. Variants in Classes D, E, F, G and O (No. XXVII). For some 15th-century variants see my contribution to *Jahrbuch*, II, and Pls. 10 and 54. This stamp differs from the others, having a much larger tree between the birds.

No. 39. Bird passant; cf. No. 9 above.

No. 40. A third palmette; cf. Nos. 12 and 20 above.

No. 41. Another eight-leaved rosette; cf. No. 21 above.

No. 42. A narrow oblong scroll or foliage stamp; cf. No. 16 above.

No. XIV, therefore, has seventeen stamps in all, only six of which are found on the other four bindings; eight others are variants of stamps used on them; three—Nos. 33, 34 and 38—are new types; it looks as if some of the stamps had changed hands and been replaced; though whether the variants on No. XIV are earlier or later than the others there is nothing to show.

[1] Mr Eric Millar, of the British Museum, has been so good as to examine no less than fourteen manuscripts for me; in none are all the elect crowned, though in the great Trinity College Apocalypse some are, while others are shown as bishops or monks—clearly "in their habits as they lived". (See the reproduction edited for the Roxburghe Club by Dr M. R. James, f. 7 b.)

[2] Reproduction in A. Goldschmidt, *Die Elfenbeinskulpturen aus der romanischen Zeit*, Berlin, 1923, Vol. III, Pl. XXVII.

[3] The stamp is interpreted thus by Weale, in Weale and Taylor, from No. XXI; but the impression is very faint and it is impossible to be quite sure of its meaning.

[4] Stone ornaments, almost exactly like this stamp, may be seen on the parish churches of Bredwardine in Herefordshire and Great Washbourn in Gloucestershire (C. E. Keyser, op. cit. figs. 27 and 13); and there is a very similar eight-leaved flower at Marseilles (R. de Lasteyrie, *L'architecture religieuse en France à l'epoque romane*, Paris, 1912, fig. 210).

[5] A carved stone ornament, closely resembling this stamp may be seen at Vienne (de Lasteyrie, op. cit. fig. 213).

APPENDIX F

On English Culture of the 12th Century and the Nationality of some Romanesque Bindings

OPINION REGARDING ROMANESQUE BINDINGS HAS COME full circle: we were brought up by Weale to believe them all to be English: and now Dr Husung, one of the latest writers to deal with them, tells us that we must no longer call any of them English *tout court*, but only 'English bindings in the French manner'. It is time to protest.

The fact is, I think, that the foreign critics are unconsciously prejudiced against this country for two easily intelligible reasons. In the first place, as bibliographers, they have been busy and familiar with the late 15th century, the period when printing was invented, or, at all events, became general: and at this time, England, impoverished and brutalized by the long barbarism of foreign and domestic warfare, was a rude and backward country, to which the light of culture filtered feebly and tardily through France and the Netherlands from Italy and south-western Germany, which were then the wealthiest and most civilized districts of Europe. In the second place, far fewer medieval works of art have survived in this country[1] than in France or Germany: our monastic libraries were dispersed at a time when the masterpieces of medieval illumination were but little regarded: and in no other country were statues and frescoes and stained glass windows so ruthlessly and systematically destroyed as in 17th-century England. The result is a general impression that England was always clumsy, always backward, always ignorant and inartistic, a reluctant scholar sitting at the feet of France.

Such a view is easier to justify than we like to admit for the 15th and 16th centuries; but it must be stated most emphatically that for the 12th century it is radically wrong, and that in the 12th century we had behind us as long a tradition of intellectual and artistic activity as any nation in the western world. For, in the Dark Ages, the homes of such civilization as lingered in Europe were not the great continental countries but the remote corners and islands—Constantinople, Cordova, Ireland, Scandinavia.[2] Between the two lastnamed lies England: is it surprising then to find manifold evidence for English proficiency in art and learning during the 9th and 10th centuries? Alcuin the Englishman was summoned by Charlemagne to direct the brief Carolingian renaissance: a school of illuminators flourished at Winchester, which was almost without a rival in Europe and was not without influence on Continental[3] art: the Manx and Northumbrian stone crosses have

[1] I am referring mainly to the smaller works of art made before 1250; as regards architecture, I find Dr Coulton quoting with approval Montalembert's statement that England is the country where, at the present day, we can most clearly see how magnificent the medieval monastic buildings were (*Art and the Reformation*, Oxford, 1928, p. 506). Yet in 12th-century architecture and sculpture we have, surely, nothing left comparable to the splendours of Arles, Moissac, Autun, Vézelay and Poitiers.

[2] The importance of early Irish civilization has long been known; it was based on the fact that Ireland was the great gold producing country of Western Europe; see Dr R. A. S. Macalister, *The Archaeology of Ireland*, 1928, p. 53. For Scandinavia see Professor A. Mawer, *The Vikings*, Cambridge, 1913; for Norse influence on Ireland, A. Walsh, *Scandinavian Relations with Ireland during the Viking Period*, Dublin, 1922; for England's debt to the Norsemen, J. W. Jeudwine, *The Manufacture of historical material*, 1916, pp. 182–98; the last-named authority calls the Norsemen "a great commercial and naval people, with a brilliant literature and a very highly developed system of law"; also, he might have added, with a very remarkable native art, which may be studied in B. Salin, *Die altgermanische Thierornamentik*, Stockholm, 1904; and in J. W. Brønsted, *Early English Ornament*, 1924. I cannot resist quoting a remark from *The Times Literary Supplement* (May 3rd, 1928):

"The Nordic invaders had no enmity at all (to ancient culture). Men who solaced their winter evenings with stories like that of Thor in Jotunheim were no foes to literature, even if they did sometimes light a camp fire with a treatise on the Monophysite heresy."

[3] Eleventh-century capitals at Cluny and Vézelay were inspired by Winchester miniatures: A. K. Porter, *Romanesque Sculpture of the Pilgrimage Roads*, Boston, 1923, Vol. I, p. 98; three 11th-century MSS., two French, one German, showing Anglo-Saxon influence, are mentioned by Mr E. G. Millar, *La miniature anglaise du Xe au XIIIe siècle*, Paris, 1926, p. 20.

long been celebrated: and there is ample testimony to the supremacy of English needlework.[1]

Nor was there any decline in the second half of the 12th century: at this period, it must be remembered, England was of great political importance as the backbone of the most powerful state in Europe: Germany was disunited; Italy torn between Guelfs and Ghibellines; Spain half-Moorish; Scandinavia decadent; and France a mere geographical expression, divided between an Angevin empire, a kingdom of Paris, and several minor principalities. Never before or since did English and Anglo-Norman ecclesiastics hold so many important foreign benefices, including the Papacy[2] itself, and the Archbishoprics[3] of Lyons, of Compsa, of Messina and of Palermo. The great John of Salisbury was Bishop of Chartres, Robert Pullen was Chancellor of the Apostolic See, and several of our compatriots, including one with the ideally English name of Thomas Brown, were in the service of King Roger of Sicily. On the other hand, very few foreigners held English Sees; the tenure of Winchester and Durham by Henry of Blois and Hugh de Puiset respectively being the exception that proves the rule, for these two ecclesiastics owed their preferment to their connection with the royal family.

In letters, it is true, the University of Paris led the world, and was largely frequented by English scholars, some of whom, like Robert of Melun, Gerard Pucelle and Adam of Bangor,[4] remained as lecturers. But learning flourished under the strong government of Henry II, which was probably the most efficient in Europe; before the end of the 12th century we had our own university[5] at Oxford; justice and bureaucracy[6] became articulate; and the King himself was a patron of literature, who delighted in the conversation of learned men. The household of Archbishop Theobald († 1161) at Canterbury was a great training ground of scholars and civil servants and was frequented by men of culture from all parts of Europe; admirable chronicles were being compiled[7] by such men as William of Malmesbury, William of Newburgh, Ralf de Diceto, and Roger of Hoveden; verses—perhaps less admirable—were being written[8] by Nigel Wireker, John de Hanville, Walter Map, Serlo of Wilton, Geoffrey de Vinsauf, and Alexander Neckham, the last-named being grammarian and man of science as well as versifier. Exeter,[9] Lincoln,[10] Peterborough, St Albans, Hexham, Salisbury and Winchester were all centres of intellectual life; and it is the considered opinion of one of the greatest of English medievalists, the late Dr Stubbs, that England at this period was a paradise of clerks, and had such a supply of writers and learned men as could be found nowhere else in Europe, except at the University of Paris.

If we turn from learning and politics to the arts, we have a similar story. The great

[1] E.g. William of Poitiers, Chronicler and Chaplain of William the Conqueror, says, "Anglicae nationis feminae multum acu et auri textura egregie, viri in omni valent artificio". Quoted by Professor G. Baldwin Brown, *The Arts in Early England*, Vol. V, p. 305, n. 1; other evidence quoted by Mr A. F. Kendrick, in the Introduction to the *Exhibition of English Embroidery*, B.F.A.C., 1905; cf. also the articles on the stole and maniple of Bishop Frithestan in the *Burlington Magazine*, Vol. XXIII, pp. 3–17 and 67–72 (April and May 1913).

[2] Nicholas Breakspear, the only English Pope, held office from 1154 to 1159 as Hadrian IV.

[3] The statements in this and the following paragraph, for which no other references are given, are taken from the two lectures by Stubbs on 'Learning and Literature at the Court of Henry II' in *Seventeen Lectures on the study of medieval and modern history*, Oxford, 1886, which according to Mr C. H. Haskins still constitute the best sketch of their subject (*Essays in Medieval History presented to T. F. Tout*, Manchester, 1925, p. 72).

[4] Nicknamed 'Parvi pontanus' or 'du petit pont' because he was one of the first to establish a school on the bridge at Paris; F. M. Powicke, *Stephen Langton*, Oxford, 1928, pp. 29 and 56.

[5] Theobald of Étampes taught at Oxford early in the 12th century, but after his time there is a gap in the records: see Sir C. E. Mallet, *History of the University of Oxford*, 1924, Vol. I, p. 20.

[6] I refer to the 'Dialogus de Scaccario' and the treatise known as 'Glanville, De legibus Angliae', for which see Pollock and Maitland, *History of English Law*, Cambridge, 1895, Vol. I, pp. 140 et seq.; the authors claim (pp. 145–6) that under Henry II England takes for a short while the lead among the states of Europe in the production of law and of a national legal literature.

[7] See F. J. E. Raby, *A History of Christian Latin Poetry*, Oxford, 1927, pp. 334 et seq.

[8] Raby, ut cit. and pp. 379–85.

[9] R. L. Poole, 'The Early lives of Robert Pullen and Nicholas Breakspear', in *Essays*, etc., *presented to T. F. Tout*, pp. 61 et seq.

[10] There was a famous theological school at Lincoln about 1180 under William of Leicester, nicknamed 'de Monte' possibly because he had taught at Ste-Geneviève; Powicke, op. cit. p. 9.

Winchester[1] Bible survives to show that the local illuminators had not lost their talent; and in the 12th century there were other flourishing schools of miniaturists at Durham, Canterbury, Westminster, Bury St Edmunds and St Albans.[2] Very few paintings on a larger scale have survived: but it is obvious that the majestic St Paul[3] at Canterbury was no isolated production since even in so remote a little church as Kempley[4] in Gloucestershire we find figures of great decorative value and dramatic power. There must have been a considerable output of stained[5] glass, though very few windows remain: Miss Longhurst[6] has called attention to our Romanesque ivories: the late Mr H. P. Mitchell[7] proved the existence of a school of English enamellers: that miracle of craftsmanship, the Gloucester[8] candlestick, shows the excellence of our metal workers, and English embroidery[9] was quite equal to the best Continental work, though the major glories of the *opus anglicanum* were still to come.

I have said enough, I hope, to show that in the second half of the 12th century England was a home of art and letters, no less likely to lead the mainland than to follow it. Coming at length to the bindings themselves, I must claim that my list and classification have limited the issues to the following:

1. Are the earliest bindings French or English?
2. What is the nationality of the 'Doubtful' group, and particularly of those bindings decorated with the tools of the great stamp cutter?

On the first question I have said my say; in my opinion, the earliest of these bindings are those composing the Winchester group; but on the second, there is more to be urged on both sides than I realized when I delivered my lecture. To take first the arguments in favour of France:

(1) There is no doubt that foreign artists and works of art came freely to England at this period: Henry of Blois[10] brought back many precious objects from his visit to Rome in 1151–2; Italian influence, if not an Italian hand, is seen by experts[11] in one of the most important manuscripts illuminated in his day at Winchester; and in the British Museum there are fragments of two remarkable enamelled plaques[12] executed for him, perhaps in England, by the great Mosan artist Godefroid de Clare. Still more noteworthy is the importation of sculptured fonts of which no less than seven,[13] executed in black Tournai marble, may still be seen at Winchester, Lincoln and elsewhere. Finally, Hugh de Puiset himself, according to the chronicler Geoffrey of Coldingham, had pillars and bases of marble brought from overseas for his projected chapel at Durham Cathedral.[14]

(2) I have next to record—what indeed has been already mentioned—the resemblance in iconography between the French and the 'Doubtful' groups; the stamps in both are much

[1] See E. G. Millar, *La miniature anglaise du Xe au XIIIe siècle*, 1926, Pls. 45–9.

[2] Millar, op. cit. p. 31; J. A. Herbert, *Illuminated Manuscripts*, 1911, p. 135.

[3] See Professors Borenius and Tristram, *English Medieval Painting*, 1926, Pl. 3.

[4] Borenius and Tristram, op. cit. Pls. 5 and 6; a few other surviving paintings of the period are mentioned by the authors, p. 4.

[5] See Herbert Read, *English Stained Glass*, 1926, p. 231. Mr Read (p. 25) accepts the interesting suggestion of W. de G. Birch that the late 12th-century drawings of the Guthlac Roll (British Museum, Harley Roll, Y. 6) are designs for stained glass medallions.

[6] *English Ivories*, 1926, pp. 15–36.

[7] In the *Burlington Magazine*, Vols. XLVII, p. 163 and XLIX, p. 161 (Oct. 1925 and Oct. 1926).

[8] In the V. and A. Museum; reproduced and discussed by J. Tavenor Perry, *Dinanderie*, 1910, p. 89 and Pl. VI.

[9] I think this is a fair inference from the remarks of Mr A. F. Kendrick, in his *Introduction to the Exhibition of English Embroidery executed prior to the middle of the XVI century, Burlington Fine Arts Club*, 1905, p. 15.

[10] J. A. Herbert, op. cit. p. 137.

[11] E. G. Millar, op. cit. p. 40.

[12] See *British Museum, A Guide to the Medieval Antiquities, etc.*, by O. M. Dalton, 1924, fig. 45 and p. 82; also the articles by H. P. Mitchell in the *Burlington Magazine*, Vol. XXXV, pp. 34 et seq. and 92 et seq.

[13] For the list and reproductions see Cecil H. Eden, *Black Tournai Fonts in England*, 1909. Messrs Prior and Gardner think that the font at Winchester was the first piece of figure sculpture in stone within the walls of the Cathedral, to which it was brought c. 1150 (*An Account of Medieval Figure-Sculpture in England*, Cambridge, 1912, pp. 148–9). In figure-sculpture we were certainly behind the French in the 12th century; their Romanesque sculpture is mainly the product of Burgundy, Languedoc, Provence and Poitou, not of Normandy.

[14] *Hist. Dunelm. Scriptores Tres*, Surtees Soc. p. 11; quoted by Professor A. Hamilton Thompson in *The National Ancient Monuments Review*, Vol. I, No. 1, 1928, pp. 30–1.

more ecclesiastical than in any of the undoubtedly English sections. The kneeling Elder is common to both; not only does he not appear on English bindings, but he seems also to be absent from English sculpture, though he is often found in France. Some other links are mentioned on p. 4, n. 1–6.

(3) Finally, the subjects of the manuscripts in these two groups agree better with each other than does either with the English group; of the fourteen manuscripts in the French group, twelve[1] are glossed books of the Bible; the figures for the great stamp cutter class are exactly the same.[2] Of the nine manuscripts in the English sections, not one is a work of this kind.

These are weighty considerations; but the counter-arguments are, in my opinion, even stronger:

1. There is evidence that books were freely exported from England to the Continent at this period; of this practice I am able to give two rather striking instances which could probably be multiplied manyfold by greater knowledge than mine:

A. In 1139, Henry of Huntingdon[3] saw at Bec the *Historia Regum Britanniae* of Geoffrey of Monmouth; "stupens inveni", says Henry, showing that he had never seen it before. The book had probably not been written more than four or five years.

B. In a 12th-century manuscript which belongs to the Bibliothèque Ste-Geneviève, Paris, is the following note, written by a Canon of Barbe-en-Ange:

"Quia autem apud Bequefort (Beckford in Gloucestershire) victualium copia erat, scriptores etiam ibi habebantur quorum opera ad nos in Normaniam mittebantur."

Mr Ernest A. Savage, indeed, from whose work *Old English Libraries* (London, Methuen and Co. n.d., p. 47, n. 1) this quotation is taken, asserts that there was a regular practice of using English houses to supply books to Norman Abbeys, a practice which partly accounts for the number of manuscripts of English workmanship now on the Continent. It is obvious that some of the manuscripts exported may have been bound, and that some of the bindings may have been decorated.

2. Technically, the work of the great stamp cutter seems closer to the stamps in the London section than to any others, and though the historiated stamps of the London section and the 'Doubtful' group are all taken from different drawings, there are very marked resemblances between some of the other stamps: between the six-leaf rosette of the Ezechiel section for example (cf. Appendix E, stamp 29) and the eight-leaf rosette of the London section; or between the rectangular ıoliage stamp shown on Pl. 6 and the similar stamps on bindings at Durham and Vienna (Nos. XIV and XXVII: see Pl. 23 and Gottlieb, Pl. 32).

The artist who worked for the London binder shared the great stamp cutter's technical skill: they are the two best craftsmen whose work is represented in the whole Romanesque family of bindings: and in view of this, it is interesting to find Mr H. S. Kingsford,[4] who catalogued

[1] The exceptions are Nos. III and XLIII.

[2] The exceptions are Nos. X and XI.

[3] Sir E. K. Chambers, *Arthur of Britain*, 1927, pp. 44–5.

[4] *Seals*, S.P.C.K. 1920, p. 54: another authority, the Rev. J. Harvey Bloom, says roundly that "the beauty of English-cut seals far surpassed those of the Continent in the thirteenth, fourteenth, and fifteenth centuries" (*English Seals*, 1906, p. xi). The fine period of seal cutting does not begin anywhere till after 1200; another consideration which supports my belief that the finest of these bindings are at all events very little earlier than that date. On the other hand, it is right to point out that the stamps on these Romanesque bindings cannot be much later than 1200. In character they belong to the 12th century; and detailed examination confirms the general impression:

1. The knights on No. XXXI wear 12th-century armour.
2. The shields have bosses (e.g. Pl. 17), and bosses were not used after about 1200 (Demay, op. cit. p. 142).
3. The architectural stamps have round, not pointed, window-heads.
4. The Elders of the Apocalypse (Appendix E, stamp 17) disappear from sculpture about 1200.
5. The bishop's crozier (Pl. 17) terminates in a simple volute; there is no sign of the fleur-de-lis introduced in the 13th century (Demay, op. cit. pp. 302–3).

the extensive collection of seals belonging to the Society of Antiquaries of London, asserting that

"In no branch of art is the high standard of English craftsmanship more in evidence than in that of seal-engraving, and the handicraft of the English artist at its highest was never surpassed, if indeed it was ever equalled, by his brother-workman on the Continent of Europe."

On technical grounds, then, we would seem to be doubly justified in claiming the great stamp-cutter for England—first on account of the excellence of his workmanship, and second on account of his relationship to the Londoner.

3. Two of the pro-French arguments have not, I think, any great weight. It is surely a mere chance that there are no glossed books in the English group, for such books must have been common in English libraries; there were a number in the collection of St Thomas à Becket[1] at Christ Church Priory, Canterbury; they constitute nearly half the 12th-century books in the Hereford[2] Cathedral Library and all but two of those bequeathed by Archdeacon Radulphus in 1195.

Nor need we lay too much stress on the argument from iconography; so many English medieval works of art have been destroyed that we are unfairly handicapped in the search for parallels; thus I have confessed ignorance of any sculptured representations in England of the four and twenty Elders of the Apocalypse, who are common in France; but Messrs Prior and Gardner[3] believe that elaborate 12th-century sculptures of the Last Judgment existed at Lincoln and York, and if they are right the Elders were very probably represented there. Again, it must be remembered that though the French stamp-types were certainly used in France, it does not follow that they were never used in England; on the contrary, the stamps reproduced on p. 6, from a binding which covered a Canterbury manuscript (No. XXXV) are distinctly 'French' in character, and so are some of the stamps on No. XIX which clothes a manuscript that may have been written in England.

4. This brings me to my last point, which is just the probability that two members at least of the 'doubtful' group—Nos. XIX and XXIII—were both written in England, and that there is nothing to show that either of them has ever crossed the Channel. I have, unfortunately, no information regarding the origin of several of the other manuscripts in the group, and until they have all been critically examined the problem of the 'doubtful' bindings cannot be solved. But at present the weight of evidence seems to be in favour of England.

I venture to add an observation which may save a future enquirer some trouble; the lettering found on some of these stamps does not help to date the bindings. The inscribed stamps are the following:

	SUBJECT OF STAMP	SECTION IN WHICH IT IS FOUND	WHERE REPRODUCED
1	Agnus Dei	E	p. 6
2	St Paul	Do.	Do.
3	Agnus Dei	F	Birkenmajer, Pl. XXVI, 5
4	St Paul	Do.	Birkenmajer, Pl. XXVI, 7
5	Do.	H	Pl. 16
6	Tullius (Cicero)	Do.	*Jahrbuch*, Pl. 4, No. 1
7	David	Do.	*Jahrbuch*, Pl. 4, No. 2
8	Samson	H (No. XXXIX)	unpublished
9	Ircus (a goat)	K (No. XLIII)	Pl. 19
10	Samson	P (No. XIX)	Pl. 29

Most of the lettering is roman, and the late W. H. St John Hope stated that the lettering on English episcopal seals changed from roman to what is usually, though incorrectly, called lombardic, about 1174 (*Proc. Soc. Ant.* Vol. XI, p. 305; for alphabets see Dalton, *British Museum, Guide, etc.* p. 157). But Mr H. S. Kingsford tells me that this is a mistake and that 12th-century seals cannot be dated from their lettering—neither then can these stamps.

The most interesting of the letters used is the L in 4 and 5 L Dr E. A. Lowe, Reader in Palaeography to the University of Oxford, tells me that this letter is found in Roman graffiti; in Christian inscriptions of Spain, Africa and Northern Italy; also in the famous Ashburnham Pentateuch (Bibl. Nat. Nouv. Acq. Lat. 2334) which is of uncertain origin; but that he had not hitherto known of its use later than the 7th century. Somehow, somewhere the form must none the less have survived; it is quite impossible to suppose that a 12th-century stamp-cutter can have revived a letter which had been obsolete for more than four hundred years.

[1] Dr M. R. James, *The Ancient Libraries of Canterbury and Dover*, 1903, pp. xli and 82–3.

[2] The Rev. Canon Bannister, *Descriptive Catalogue of the MSS. in the Hereford Cathedral Library*, Hereford, 1927, Introduction by Dr M. R. James, pp. iii and iv.

[3] Op. cit. pp. 80–1, and 212–3.

APPENDIX G

An Attempted Classification of Oxford 15th-Century Bindings, based on Mr Strickland Gibson's Monograph

GROUP	NUMBERS IN MR GIBSON'S LIST	REPRODUCTIONS IN GIBSON	STAMPS IN THE GROUP
A	1–7, 10–12, 21–3, 26–8, 30–1	Pls. I–V, VIII, XII–XIV, XVII and XXXI	1–18, 27–32,[1] 52–59, 72–81
B	8	VI	19–21
C	9	VII	22–26
D	13	—	33–4
E	14	—	37–9
F	15	—	40
G	16	XXXII	35, 36, 41–3, and one similar to 68
H	17–20	IX–XI	44–51
I	24–5	XV–XVI	60–71
K	32	XVIII	82–87
L[2]	33	—	88–90

Detailed list of Group A, showing the links between the different sections:

	DATE, ETC.	NUMBER IN MR GIBSON'S LIST	REPRODUCTION	STAMPS
I	Late 13th-century MS.	6	—	6–14
II	Early 14th-century MS.	28	—	18, 55, 73, 77–9
III	n.d. MS.	2	G, Pl. II	6–9
IV	n.d.[3] MS.	7	G, Pl. V	5, 17, 18
V	n.d. MS.	10	G, Pl. XXXI	16, 27–9
VI	n.d. MS.	12	—	27, 30–1
VII	n.d. MS.	26	—	72–5
VIII	c. 1450[4] MS.	Not in G	See Pl. 35	1, 2, 4, 80
IX	1460 MS.	1	G, Pl. I	1, 2, 6
X	? before 1462 MS.	3	G, Pl. III	6, 10–15
XI	before 1470 MS.	4	G, Pl. IV	3–6, 11, 13–16
XII	1471 MS.	5	—	3, 6, 11, 13–15
XIII	1475, Venice	11	G, Pl. VIII	16, 27
XIV	1478, Venice	22	G, Pl. XII	52–5
XV	1480, Venice	27	—	55, 72, 76
XVI	1480, London	30	G, Pl. XVII	80, 81
XVII	1480,[5] Venice	Not in G	—	4, 80
XVIII	1482 MS.	21	—	11, 52–4
XIX	1482, Oxford	23	G, Pls. XIII and XIV; see Pl. 36	52–3, 56–9
XX	1482, Venice	31	—	4, 80
XXI	1488–9[6] MS.	Not in G	—	55, 80, 81 and one not in G
XXII	n.d. (an empty binding)[7]	Not in G	—	1, 2 and three not in G

[1] Stamp No. 32 is mentioned by Mr Gibson (p. 19, No. 12) as occurring with 27 on a binding at Durham.

[2] To this list should perhaps be added the binding reproduced as Pl. I of *Thirty Bindings* (First Edition Club, London, 1926) which was rather too light-heartedly described as "undoubtedly an Oxford binding".

[3] Nos. IV, VIII, IX, XI, XII, XVI, XVII, XX, XXI and XXII are decorated with the archaic stamps, Nos. 1–5 and 80: see notes to Pl. II, *Bindings in Cambridge Libraries.*

[4] British Museum, Egerton MS. 2892.

[5] Corpus Christi College, Cambridge: Gaselee 46; see Pl. 27, stamps *a* and *b*.

[6] Register of the Guild of the Holy Cross, Stratford-on-Avon; the MS. cost 2*s*. 10*d*. to bind in 1488–9 (information from Mr F. C. Wellstood).

[7] Weale, R. 40.

CLASSIFICATION OF OXFORD 15TH-CENTURY BINDINGS

In my notes on Pl. II, *Bindings in Cambridge Libraries*, I have briefly set out the proofs that the ten bindings with the archaic stamps (Gibson, Nos. 1–5 and 80) are of Oxford workmanship: a similar statement, compiled from Mr Gibson's book, regarding the other twelve bindings in Group A, may be useful:

1. No. II was deposited in 1482 in the Chichele Chest.
2. No. V covers a cartulary of Osney Abbey.
3. No. X covers a MS. written by J. Goolde, a Fellow of Magdalen College.
4. No. XIV was given to Magdalen College by William Rydyall, who apparently bequeathed his books to the College in 1494–5.
5. No. XVIII was written by Richard Rawlyns who was probably a Fellow of Merton College, 1480.

APPENDIX H

English Cut Leatherwork, 1300–1500

THE SURVIVING ENGLISH CUT LEATHERWORK THAT I HAVE studied[1] falls into two classes: the first of these I have already mentioned as resembling the work of the 'Scales binder' (see p. 18). It is represented by collections in the British, Guildhall and London Museums of objects such as shoes, pouches, dagger sheaths, saddlery, etc.; the specimens shown on Pl. 40 are typical of the group as a whole.

The second class consists of a number of boxes, mostly cylindrical[2], which are widely scattered. Those known to me are the following:

	OWNERSHIP	REFERENCE	REPRODUCTION
1	Church of St Agnes, Cawston, Norfolk	*Proc. Soc. Ant.*, 2nd Series, Vol. XIV (1893), pp. 246–52	*Proc. Soc. Ant.*, ut cit.
2	Unknown; said to have been found at the Church of St Chad, Dunholme, Lincs.	Ibid. p. 252	Unpublished
3	Church of St Neot's, Cornwall	Ibid.	Do.
4	Church of St Peter, Barrowden, Rutland	Ibid.	Do.
5	Chapel of the Pyx, Westminster Abbey	Ibid.	Do.
6	Church of Moulton, Norfolk	Ibid. Vol. XVII (1899), p. 367	See Pl. 41
7	Museum, York	*Journ. Brit. Arch. Assoc.*, Vol. III, p. 123	*Journ. Brit. Arch. Assoc.*, ut. cit.
8	Public Record[3] Office (?)	*Arch. Journ.*, Vol. XXVIII, p. 138	*Arch. Journ.*, ut cit., p. 137
9	Church of Lanivet, Cornwall	Ibid., p. 138	Ibid.
10 & 11	Public Record[4] Office	Ibid., p. 138. *P.R.O. Museum Catalogue*, 1926, p. 72, Nos. VII A and B	See Pl. 41 *a*
12	British Museum (formerly Little Welnetham Church, Suffolk)	*British Museum, A Guide to the Medieval Antiquities*, by O. M. Dalton, 1924, p. 60	*B.M. Guide*, fig. 172

I have not seen all these boxes; but so far as I can judge from those I have seen, and from descriptions and reproductions of those I have not, they are all, with one exception, decorated very much like the boxes shown on Pls. 41 and 41 *a*. They are good second class work, as much above the crudities of the Scales binder and his fellows, as they are below the masterpieces of contemporary Continental workers.

The exception is No. 1, which was described at length for the Society of Antiquaries by the late Sir A. W. Franks, and assigned by him to the 14th century, whereas all the other boxes date from the 15th or the 16th. Its decoration is entirely heraldic, consisting of the arms or badges of various East Anglian families, and judging from the reproductions it is vastly superior to all its fellow-boxes. Indeed, it is at least equal to the finest German work of the 14th century, thus furnishing one more proof of the excellence of English art in 1300, while the other boxes mark its decline in the two following centuries.

[1] What seems to have been a very interesting collection of cut or stamped leather is described in the *Catalogue of the Museum of London Antiquities, collected by Charles Roach Smith, printed for the subscribers only*, 1850, pp. 123–33, with reproductions. I owe my knowledge of the catalogue to Mr J. B. Caldecott; but unfortunately I have been unable to trace the collection, which judging from the few pieces reproduced must have been of considerable importance.

[2] The exceptions, so far as I know, are No. 7, which is a shallow round box, and Nos. 10 and 11, which are rectangular.

[3] This box is not discoverable now.

[4] These boxes contained indentures relating to Westminster Abbey.

Two other published boxes have been described as English:

1. The box illustrated below[1], which was made for the celebrated glass cup known as "The Luck of Edenhall". Mr W. B. Honey, who published the box in the *Burlington Magazine*,

[1] Reproduced from the *Burlington Magazine*, June 1927, by kind permission of its owner, Sir Courtenay Musgrave, Bt., and of the proprietors of the *Burlington Magazine*.

thought that it was either English or French; it is quite unlike any work known to me which is certainly English, but whether it be French or not I am unable to judge.

2. A case for writer's implements, dating from the early 16th century, which was formerly in the Spitzer collection, has been called[1] English because it is decorated with the English Royal arms. But it is easy to quote works of art[2] adorned in this fashion by foreigners during the Tudor period, and there is nothing else to suggest that the box is of English workmanship. On the contrary, it is gilt and painted, and therefore probably Continental, such ornament being uncommon, if not unknown, on English leatherwork of the period.

[1] In *La Collection Spitzer*, Paris et Londres, 1891, Vol. II, *Cuirs*, Pl. III.

[2] E.g. Royal MS. 16. F. II, see p. 25, n. 3; and two Flemish damasks illustrated by R. Glazier, *Historic Textile Fabrics*, 1923, Pls. 75 and 76. A fine Flemish cut leather box, made in 1468 to hold the marriage crown of Margaret of York, is decorated with the arms of Burgundy and England, quartered. See F. Bock, *Die Kleinodien des heiligen römischen Reiches*, Vienna, 1864, p. 213.

APPENDIX J

Additional 15th-Century English Bindings and a list of English 'small-stamp' Binderies working before 1510

I. Pl. 32 *a*. An English monastic binding

Title, etc. Sermons of John Lensean, etc. MS. on vellum, 15th century.

Ownership. Lincoln Cathedral Library.

Pressmark. B. 6. 9: No. 231 of the catalogue of the MSS. in the Chapter Library by the Rev. R. M. Woolley, D.D., Oxford 1927.

Size. 181 × 126 mm.

Material, etc. Chocolate coloured leather.

Previous ownership. The Cistercian Abbey of St Mary, Jervaulx, Yorks.

Remarks. The one stamp used on this humble little binding no doubt represents the Virgin, with orb and sceptre, and may be regarded as the ownership stamp of the monastery. It seemed worth while to reproduce it, in view of the rarity of English stamped monastic bindings; a few are assigned by Weale to Tavistock (R. 41), Salisbury (R. 42) and Oxford (R. 47), but none has any distinctive stamp till we reach the 16th-century products of Old Bokenham (R. 66) and Glastonbury (R. 184), and the localization of the earlier specimens is far from certain. English undecorated monastic bindings, usually of rough deerskin, are common enough; I have seen a fine series in Worcester Cathedral Library, and an example from Reading Abbey on Egerton MS. 2204 in the British Museum is excellently reproduced by Dr M. R. James in *Abbeys*, 1926, p. 14.

II. Pl. 38. An English 15th-century binding. ? London, ? c. 1470

Title, etc. Albertus, *de caelo et mundo*, etc. English MS. on vellum, 15th century.

Ownership. Pembroke College, Cambridge.

Pressmark. MS. 204.

Size. 320 × 235 mm.

Material, etc. Brown calf: five bands; the binding, the lower cover of which is very dilapidated, has been removed from its manuscript, which is now in a modern binding.

Remarks. There can be no doubt of the nationality of this binding; it comes from an English manuscript which seems never to have been out of the country. Dating and closer localization are much more difficult; I have proposed London because the stamp forming the outer border very closely resembles a stamp similarly used by the 'Scales binder' (see *Bindings in Cambridge Libraries*, Pl. VI); my date is suggested by the arrangement of the stamps, which is of the type found at Salisbury, Oxford and London soon after 1460. But neither argument is conclusive: stamps and stamp types were migratory in the 15th century; Mr E. P. Goldschmidt (p. 124) quotes the use of South-German types at Lübeck; in England we find Caxton's binder importing stamps from Bruges (p. 19) and the Rebus binder using a round pelican which is very similar to a Cambridge stamp as well as a nosegay which resembles a Westminster stamp (cf. the reproductions, p. 23 and Pls. 38 and 43). Nor is the date less dubious; for though no other pattern, so far as I know, is found on English bindings before about 1475, this linear arrangement survived to a much later period. Mr E. P. Goldschmidt has a French example on the covers of a book printed in 1496 (No. 40, p. 167), and there is a specimen in the Peterhouse Library on the binding of a copy of Henry VIII, *Assertio Septem Sacramentorum*, printed in 1521 (Pressmark Q. 3. 1).

APPENDIX J

III. Pl. 50. English or Netherlands binding, c. 1490

Title, etc. Geraldus Odonis, *Super librum ethicorum*, Brescia, 1482.

Ownership. Lincoln Cathedral Library.

Pressmark. Inc. 51.

Size. 310 × 186 mm.

Material, etc. Very dark brown leather, rebacked.

Remarks. I have spoken of this binding in my remarks on Pl. XIII of *Bindings in Cambridge Libraries*; its decorative scheme and stamps are so like those of the 'Demon' and 'Unicorn' binders that it seems to me very likely to come from a Cambridge bindery, though, strictly speaking, even its nationality is uncertain. It is probable that Cambridge supplied Lincoln with a good many bound books in the 15th century; three of the works by the 'Unicorn binder' are in the Cathedral library, and another belonged at an early date to a Lincolnshire family (No. XVIII A of the list given with Pl. XIV of *Bindings in Cambridge Libraries*: cf. Quaritch catalogue, 412 (December 1927), No. 124).

It can be proved that there were at least eighteen binderies working in England between 1450 and the accession of Henry VIII in 1509 at which stamped leather bindings were produced, namely:

1. Canterbury: Pl. 33.

2. Salisbury: Pl. 34.

3 and 4. Oxford.

- 3. An archaizing binder: Pls. 35 and 36, see Appendix G, group A.
- 4. Rood and Hunte's binder: Pl. 37, see Appendix G, group H.

5–7. London and Westminster.

- 5. The 'Scales binder': Pl. 39.
- 6. Caxton's binder: Pls. 42–44.
- 7. The 'Indulgence binder': Pl. 45.

8 and 9. Cambridge.

- 8. The 'Demon binder': Pl. 46.
- 9. The 'Unicorn binder': Pls. 47–49.

10 and 11. Possibly Cambridge.

- 10. G.W. or W.G.: Pl. 51.
- 11. The 'Huntsman binder': see *Bindings in Cambridge Libraries*, Pl. XV, section D.

12–17. Uncertain—possibly all London.

- 12. The binder represented by Pl. 38.
- 13. The 'Rebus binder': p. 23.
- 14. The 'Dragon binder': Pl. 52.
- 15. The 'Greyhound binder': Pl. 53.
- 16. A second archaizing binder: Pl. 54.
- 17. Another binder represented by a single work only, which covers Bodley's copy of Henry Parker, *Dives and Pauper*, London (Pynson) 1493. The cover is divided into the usual lozenge-shaped compartments, in each of which is the stamp reproduced. The book was owned in 1500 by John Adeson.

18. St Mary's Abbey, Jervaulx: Pl. 32 *b*.

Apart from No. 18, to the date of which I have no clue, these bindings fall into three distinct chronological groups:

A. Nos. 1 to 3, 5 and possibly 12: from about 1460.
B. Nos. 4, 6 and 7: from about 1475.
C. Nos. 8 to 11 and 13 to 17: from about 1485, or later.

In addition, there are the following possibilities:

19. A second Salisbury binder: Weale, R. 42.

20. A Tavistock binder: Weale, R. 41.

21–30. Ten more Oxford binders: Appendix G, groups B–G, and I–L, and *Thirty Bindings*, Pl. I.

31. A Cambridge binder: Pl. 50.

32. A Winchester binder: Weale, R. 51–2.

33. Another binder who may have worked at Cambridge. The Rev. G. A. Schneider told me of the following bindings by him, all in the Library of Gonville and Caius College:

I. 1485: Strasburg (Inc. 5).
II. 1495: Venice (Inc. 46).
III. n.d.: Basle (Inc. 77).

Four tools are used on these bindings:

1. Lozenge shaped: a crowned double-headed eagle[1]; for two very similar stamps, see Pl. 51 and Weale, R. 374.

2. Square: a running stag; closely resembling a stamp used by the 'Demon binder': see *Bindings in Cambridge Libraries*, Pl. XIII and Pl. XV, No. 12.

3. Circular: a fleur-de-lis.

4. Lozenge shaped: a small four-pointed star.

At present the only reason for supposing him to have worked at Cambridge, or even in England, is the fact that II contains an inscription stating that it was bought at Stourbridge Fair in 1497. On Mr E. P. Goldschmidt's principles (see his pp. 36–39 and 118) this would indicate that the bindings are of local workmanship; but one entry is hardly sufficient to prove this, and unluckily I learnt of these bindings too late to search for examples in other Cambridge Libraries.

Even if we take what would, in my opinion, be an absurdly rigorous view, and refuse to place any of the possibilities in England, we must allow for unidentified binderies and destroyed bindings; there can hardly have been less than thirty binderies turning out decorated bindings in England during the sixty years under examination, and there may have been twice that number, though not, I think, many more.

[1] The stamps probably come from Antwerp, the double-headed eagle being recorded by Weale associated with a stamp of the town arms.

APPENDIX K

Unbound Books in Medieval Libraries

THAT UNBOUND MANUSCRIPTS OFTEN REPOSED FOR YEARS on the shelves of medieval libraries; and that, in consequence, a medieval binding may be ten, twenty, fifty, a hundred years or more later than the manuscript it covers; is a fact which, though well known[1], is constantly disregarded; it can be proved in several different ways:—

1. Books are often described in contemporary catalogues as being 'in quaternis'[2], or 'in quaternionibus', or 'tout en cayers'. True, I have found twenty-four[3] such descriptions only among 1236 books in the Louvre Library, but they are common in the old St Gall[4] catalogue; and six books were unbound out of twenty-seven[5] bequeathed in 1492 to the library of Notre-Dame by Louis de Beaumont, Bishop of Paris.

2. Some manuscripts contain entries proving that they were bound long after they were written: thus an episcopal register[6] at Breslau though begun in 1368 was not bound till 1475, nor a collection of 12th-century decrees at Weingarten till 1338.

3. The regulations of some corporate libraries forbid books to be lent in quires for copying —e.g. Magdalen[7] and Brasenose Colleges, Oxford, and Pembroke College, Cambridge.

It is also necessary to remember that books might be rebound in the Middle Ages for two distinct reasons, apart from ordinary wear and tear:—

1. Books were often bound in limp parchment, which might easily have to be replaced by something more solid; of the first fifteen books in a fragmentary[8] catalogue of the library of Christ Church Priory, Canterbury, c. 1170, seven are described as 'in pargameno', against five 'in asseribus', one 'in rubeo corio' and two unspecified; but this, I must admit, seems an unusually high proportion of parchment-bound books; in the Louvre catalogue I have counted eighty-two only, or about one in fifteen.

2. Books already bound might be taken out of their bindings for transport and rebound on arrival; the Franciscan Adam de Marisco[9], writing about the middle of the 13th century to William of Nottingham, Provincial Minister of the English Franciscans, requests the return of certain books and adds—

"Bene, si placet, faciatis componi libros praenominatos, ablatis asseribus, in panno cerato."

This is a particularly interesting entry, for it suggests that the practice of forwarding books in sheets was adopted by the early printers from their predecessors, the dealers in manuscripts; from the same source, no doubt, they took their method of charging for books by the quire, this being the natural basis for the remuneration[10] of scribes.

[1] Dr Gottlieb is the latest writer to call attention to it, in his review of Dr Bollert's book on 14th-century cut leather bindings; *Göttingischen gelehrten Anzeigen*, 1927, Nos. 9 and 10, pp. 337–46.

[2] W. Wattenbach, *Das Schriftwesen im Mittelalter*, Second Edition, Leipzig, 1875, p. 330.

[3] *Inventaire...fait en l'année 1373 par Gilles Mallet*, Paris, De Bure, 1836.

[4] Wattenbach, op. cit.

[5] The list is given by A. Franklin, *Recherches sur la bibliothèque publique de l'église N.-D. de Paris*, Paris, 1863, pp. 58–62.

[6] Both examples quoted by Wattenbach, op. cit.

[7] See Ernest A. Savage, *Old English Libraries*, n.d., p. 168.

[8] Dr M. R. James, *The Ancient Libraries of Canterbury and Dover*, 1903, p. 7.

[9] *Monumenta Franciscana*, 1858, Vol. I, pp. 377–8.

[10] Cf. the accounts quoted by Mr Falconer Madan, *Books in Manuscript*, 1893, pp. 43 and 44.

ADDENDA

p. 4, n. 4. *The Tiger.* It is unfortunately not quite certain that this animal is a tiger, though it resembles tigers drawn by medieval artists and is in the attitude in which a tiger is occasionally shown: but to make the identification certain it should be looking at a small round mirror. When the hunter had stolen the tiger's cubs, the tiger—or rather the tigress—pursued him with incredible speed; on the point of being overtaken the hunted hunter threw down a mirror. Seeing her own reflexion the tigress thought that the face was that of one of her lost cubs, and before she had discovered her mistake, the hunter was far away. Overtaken again, he threw down another mirror; again the tigress paused; again she pursued, and was again beguiled; thus, if he had plenty of mirrors, the hunter got safely home! An admirable device truly, though it does not provide for the possibility that the tigress might not look at the mirrors at all; but perhaps the medieval scientist would retort that the objection is absurd, and that no female can ever pass a mirror without looking at it (see Francis Bond, *Misericords*, 1910, pp. 26–7 and G. C. Druce in *Archaeologia Cantiana*, XXVIII, 363). It occurs to me that the stamp may represent the she-wolf filling her belly with clay, as she was wont to do when she could get no other food: but when she killed, she put her paw in her mouth and vomited the clay (E. P. Evans, *Animal Symbolism in Ecclesiastical Architecture*, 1896, p. 151). I can find no confirmation of Dr Haseloff's conjecture that the animal may be a bear, which is generally shown either dancing, or—literally—licking its cubs into shape (see Haseloff, p. 511, *Jahrbuch*, p. 6, n. 5 and Pl. 4, stamp 14).

p. 6. *Stamped bindings at Canterbury.* The attribution of No. XXXV to Canterbury is obviously very speculative: it is impossible to say that the manuscript was written there, and, as I have shown on p. 33, several different binderies might be represented in an early monastic library. I should not venture to advance it even as a hypothesis were not Canterbury *à priori* a likely home for a binder using metal stamps.

p. 17, n. 3. *The stamp of two birds drinking from a cup.* The two birds are probably peacocks: if so, their origin is classical, not oriental. The peacock was the bird of Juno: hence of the Roman Empresses: and as these ladies achieved immortality on their apotheosis, the peacock became an emblem of eternal life, first Pagan, then Christian. In Byzantine art it is common: and in the whole range of Byzantine sculpture hardly anything is more beautiful, says Mr Bond, than the two peacocks which may be seen in chancel screens at Brescia and Ancona, drinking from a chalice the sacramental wine of eternal life (Francis Bond, *Misericords*, 1910, p. 6).

pp. 20–1. *The stamp of a crane attacking a quadruped.* It is possible that this stamp does not come from either of the sources that I have suggested. A crane-like bird may be seen standing on, and pecking the back of a bull in a very fine initial T of an early 12th century manuscript in the Bibliothèque de la Ville, Dijon (see C. Oursel, *La miniature du XIIe siècle à l'abbaye de Cîteaux*, Dijon, 1926, Pl. XXXII and p. 36). A crow perched in similar fashion on a sheep sometimes illustrates Aesop's Fable of the Sheep and the Crow (e.g. Pynson's edition, 1497: reproduction in Quaritch catalogue 369, April 1922, Pl. I).

p. 37. *The descent of the woutre from the wivre.* The serpentine origin of the woutre appears clearly from his reluctance to attack the naked. For one of the most astounding facts in the history of the serpent is his omission to bite Adam and Eve, and every medieval schoolboy knew that this failure was due to the nudity of our first parents: being unclad by so much as a fig-leaf they were free from the taint of the world and immune from the assault of the Evil One (see Francis Bond, *Misericords*, 1910, p. 41).

p. 37. *The nude figure*, stamp No. 9. If my explanation of the stamp proves untenable, I suggest that the figure may be copied from some drawing of man as the Microcosm, such as we find in the works of the 12th century authoresses Hildegard of Bingen and Herrade de Landsberg (see Charles Singer, *From Magic to Science*, 1928, figs. 103 and 105). But this leaves the animal (stamp No. 11) unexplained.

p. 46. *Differences in design and similarity in technique between the London stamps and those of the great stamp-cutter.* Quite possibly the drawings for the two sets of stamps are the work of different artists. It is not probable that the stamp-cutters, who like the seal-cutters were presumably goldsmiths, designed their own stamps: they are more likely to have worked from drawings supplied by painters. Thus in the 14th century the famous artist Jean Pucelle was paid three sols for designing the great seal of the brotherhood of St Jacques-aux-Pèlerins at Paris (Marcel Poète, *Les primitifs parisiens*, Paris, 1904, p. 29). Similarly we find that the miniatures of manuscripts illuminated at Paris in the later Middle Ages are often the work of copyists, who elaborated more or less skilfully the rough sketches of the *chef d'atelier* (see Henry Martin, *Les Miniaturistes français*, Paris, 1906, pp. 100 et seq.). Further light on the methods of medieval craftsmen is thrown by the history of the weaving of the famous tapestries in the Cathedral of Angers. The Duke of Anjou borrowed a manuscript of the Apocalypse from his brother Charles V. From the miniatures therein the painter Jean de Bruges made large cartoons for which he was paid in 1378. The weaving was then begun by Nicholas Bataille but was not finished till the middle of the 15th century (Marcel Aubert, Decorative and Industrial Arts, in *The Legacy of the Middle Ages*, Oxford, 1926, p. 138).

In short, we can hardly be far wrong if we think of these Romanesque stamps as designed by artists, engraved by goldsmiths, and generally mis-used by binders.

I should like to add what must for the present at all events be my final word on the nationality of the 'Doubtful' Romanesque bindings, and indeed of the whole Romanesque family, except the two German bindings. I have said (p. 11) that the first-named "came into existence not far from the Straits of Dover, in S.E. England or in Northern France". This, at all events, still seems to me to be certain, and though, in my opinion, as I have said (p. 47) the balance of the evidence is in favour of England the scales lie very evenly, and some of my readers may well consider that my view of their alignment is incorrect; perhaps it will never be possible to say with certainty in which country the 'Doubtful' group originated. Hence they add a further proof of the close artistic relations which existed in the 12th century between the two shores of the English Channel.

Mr Bernard Rackham, writing in the *Burlington Magazine* for January, 1928 (p. 41) on the early stained glass of Canterbury Cathedral, observes that "The *general* similarity of the Canterbury work to the French glass-paintings of their age cannot be denied, and accords with the view that Southern England and Northern France at that time formed one region of art, with slight local variations". Mr Eric Millar (*La miniature anglaise du Xe au XIIIe siècle*, Paris, 1926, p. 52) is only deterred from claiming the Ingeburge Psalter at Chantilly for England, by the crested and prevailing shade of Delisle who had described it as French. The famous ivory carving in the Victoria and Albert Museum of the Adoration of the Magi is assigned by Dr A. Goldschmidt to Northern France, and is claimed by Miss M. H. Longhurst for England (see Victoria and Albert Museum, *Catalogue of Carvings in Ivory*, Part I, 1927, pp. 87–8). Finally, Messrs Borenius and Tristram, speaking of the intimate relations between England and France at this period say that "on the analogy of what has been called the 'Style of the Danube' in the history of German painting, one feels inclined, in certain instances, to speak of a 'Style of the English Channel', thus emphasising what is common property rather than accentuating the local differences" (*English Mediaeval Painting*, 1926, p. 10).

May we not apply this admirable suggestion to our problem, and say that to the School of the English Channel belong not only the 'Doubtful' bindings, but the French and English groups as well? I would not even except the Durham section, the stamps on which have all the characteristics of the other founts and may well have been brought from the South of England.

PLATES

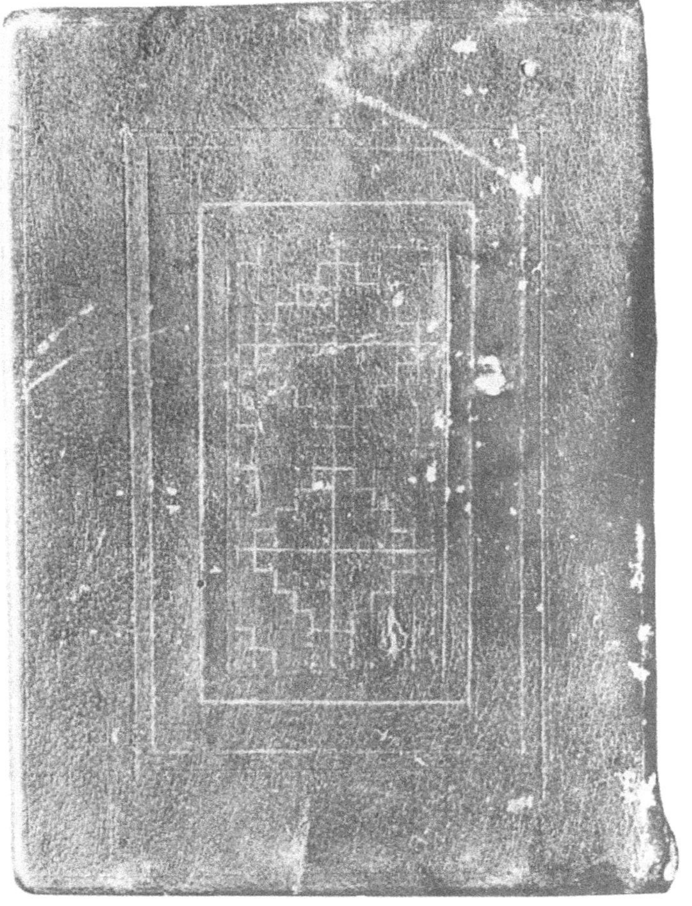

1

PLATE I. A 7th-century Northumbrian binding. See pp. 1–2.

STONYHURST COLLEGE, LANCS.

PLATE 2. Satchel of the Book of Armagh (front). See Appendix A, p. 26, No. 1.

TRINITY COLLEGE, DUBLIN

PLATE 3. Back of the satchel shown on Pl. 2.

PLATE 4. A Romanesque binding: class A (Winchester). List p. 29, No. v. *Upper cover.*

SOCIETY OF ANTIQUARIES, LONDON

PLATE 5. Lower cover of the binding shown on Pl. 4.

PLATE 6. A Romanesque binding: class B (London). List p. 29, No. XVII. *Upper cover.*

PUBLIC RECORD OFFICE, LONDON

PLATE 7. Lower cover of the binding shown on Pl. 6.

PLATE 8. A Romanesque binding: class B (London). List p. 30, No. XXIV. *Lower cover.*

PLATE 9. A Romanesque binding: class C (Durham). List p. 29, No. VII. *Upper cover.*

CATHEDRAL LIBRARY, DURHAM

PLATE 10. A Romanesque binding: class D (? Oxford). List p. 29, No. XVI. *Upper cover.* BRITISH MUSEUM, LONDON

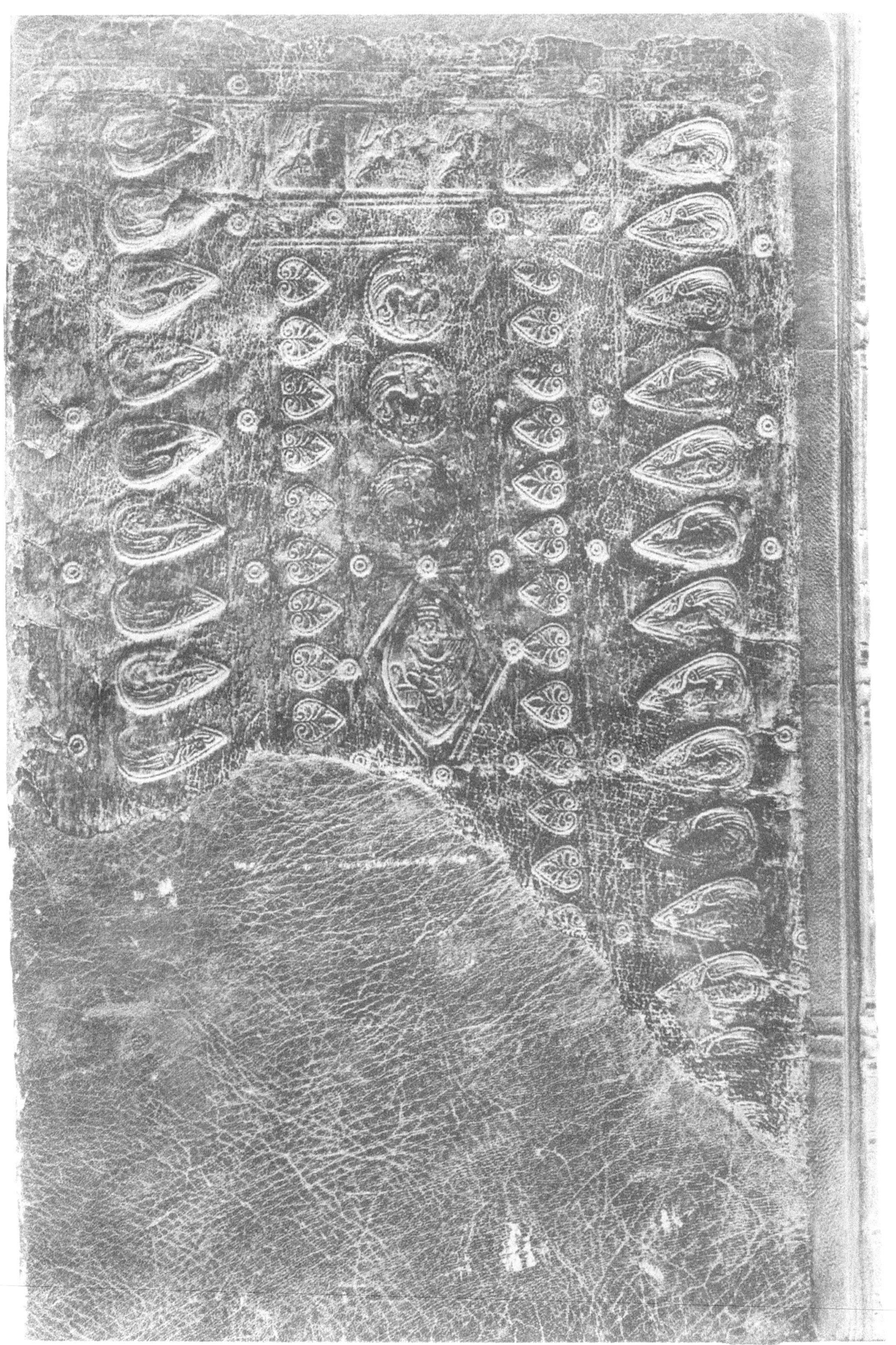

PLATE 11. Lower cover of the binding shown on Pl. 10.

PLATE 12. A Romanesque binding: class F (French). List p. 31, No. XLII. *Upper cover.*

BIBLIOTHÈQUE DE LA VILLE, TROYES

PLATE 13. Lower cover of the binding shown on Pl. 12.

PLATE 14. A Romanesque binding: class G (French). List p. 31, No. XL. *Upper cover.* BIBLIOTHÈQUE DE LA VILLE, TROYES

PLATE 15. Lower cover of the binding shown on Pl. 14.

PLATE 16. A Romanesque binding: class H (French).
List p. 30, No. XXXVI.

ADMONT MONASTERY, STYRIA

PLATE 17. A Romanesque binding: class K (French). List p. 31, No. XLI. *Upper cover.* BIBLIOTHÈQUE DE LA VILLE, TROYES

PLATE 18. A Romanesque binding: class K (French). List p. 31, No. XLIII. See Appendix D, pp. 36–8. *Upper cover.*

BIBLIOTHÈQUE DE LA VILLE, TROYES

PLATE 19. Lower cover of the binding shown on Pl. 18.

PLATE 20. A Romanesque binding: class L (nationality doubtful). List p. 29, No. XI. *Upper cover.*

CATHEDRAL LIBRARY, HEREFORD

PLATE 21. Lower cover of the binding shown on Pl. 20.

PLATE 21 *a*. A Romanesque binding: class L (nationality doubtful). List p. 29, No. XII. *Upper cover.*

CATHEDRAL LIBRARY, DURHAM

PLATE 21 *b*. Lower cover of the binding shown on Pl. 21 *a*.

PLATE 22. A Romanesque binding: class M (nationality doubtful). List p. 29, No. XIV. *Upper cover.* CATHEDRAL LIBRARY, DURHAM

PLATE 23. Lower cover of the binding shown on Pl. 22.

PLATE 24. Rubbing of a Romanesque binding: class M (nationality doubtful). List p. 29, No. x. *Upper cover.*

? BIBLIOTHÈQUE MAZARINE, PARIS

PLATE 25. Lower cover of the binding shown on Pl. 24.

PLATE 26. A Romanesque binding: class M (nationality doubtful). List p. 30, No. XXIII. *Lower cover.* PEMBROKE COLLEGE, CAMBRIDGE

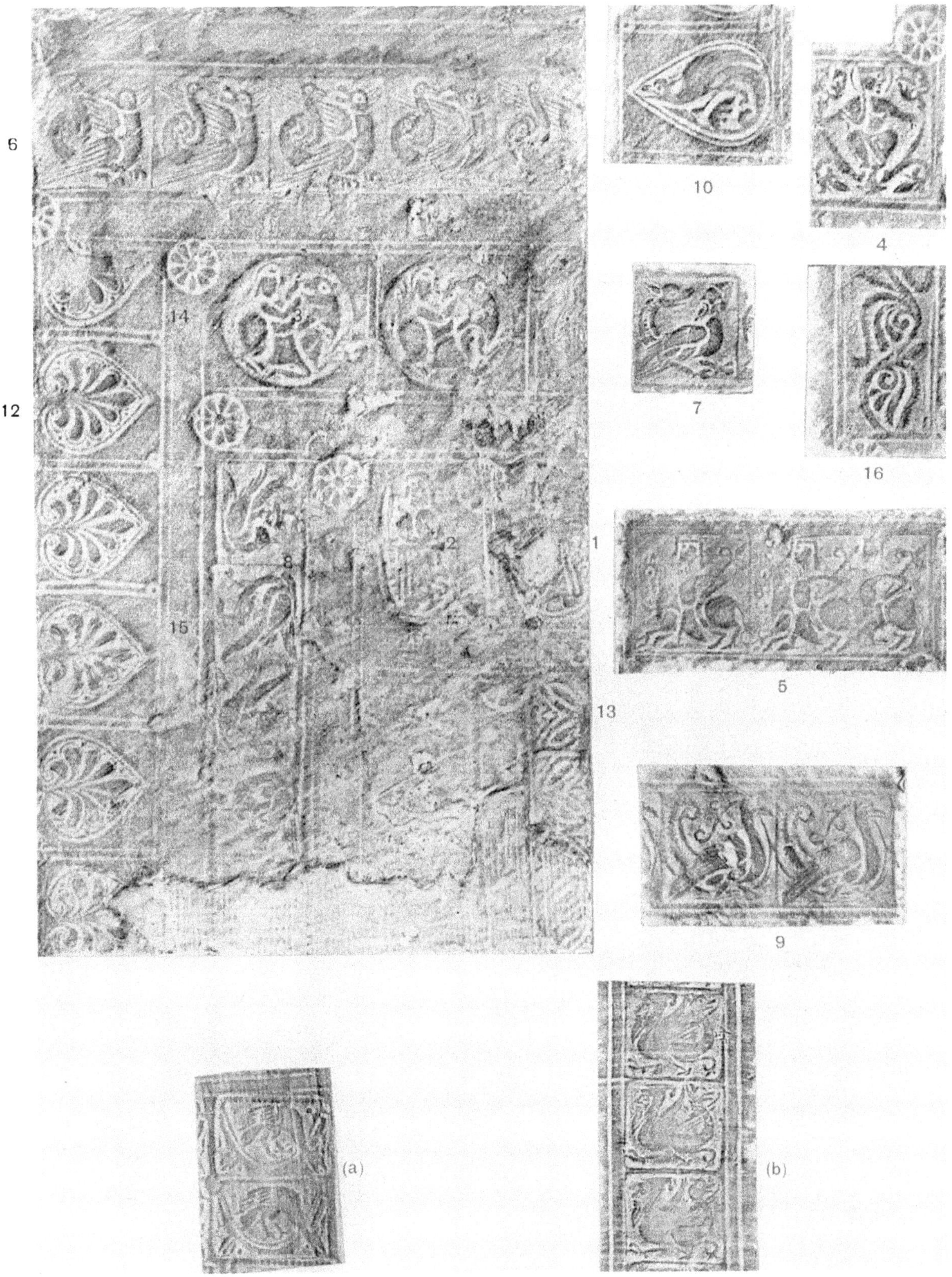

PLATE 27. Romanesque stamps; Nos. 1–16 from the two covers of the binding shown on Pl. 26. Nos. *a* and *b* used at Oxford in the fifteenth century: see p. 17.

PLATE 28. A Romanesque binding: class N (nationality doubtful). List p. 31, No. XXXVIII.

ADMONT MONASTERY, STYRIA

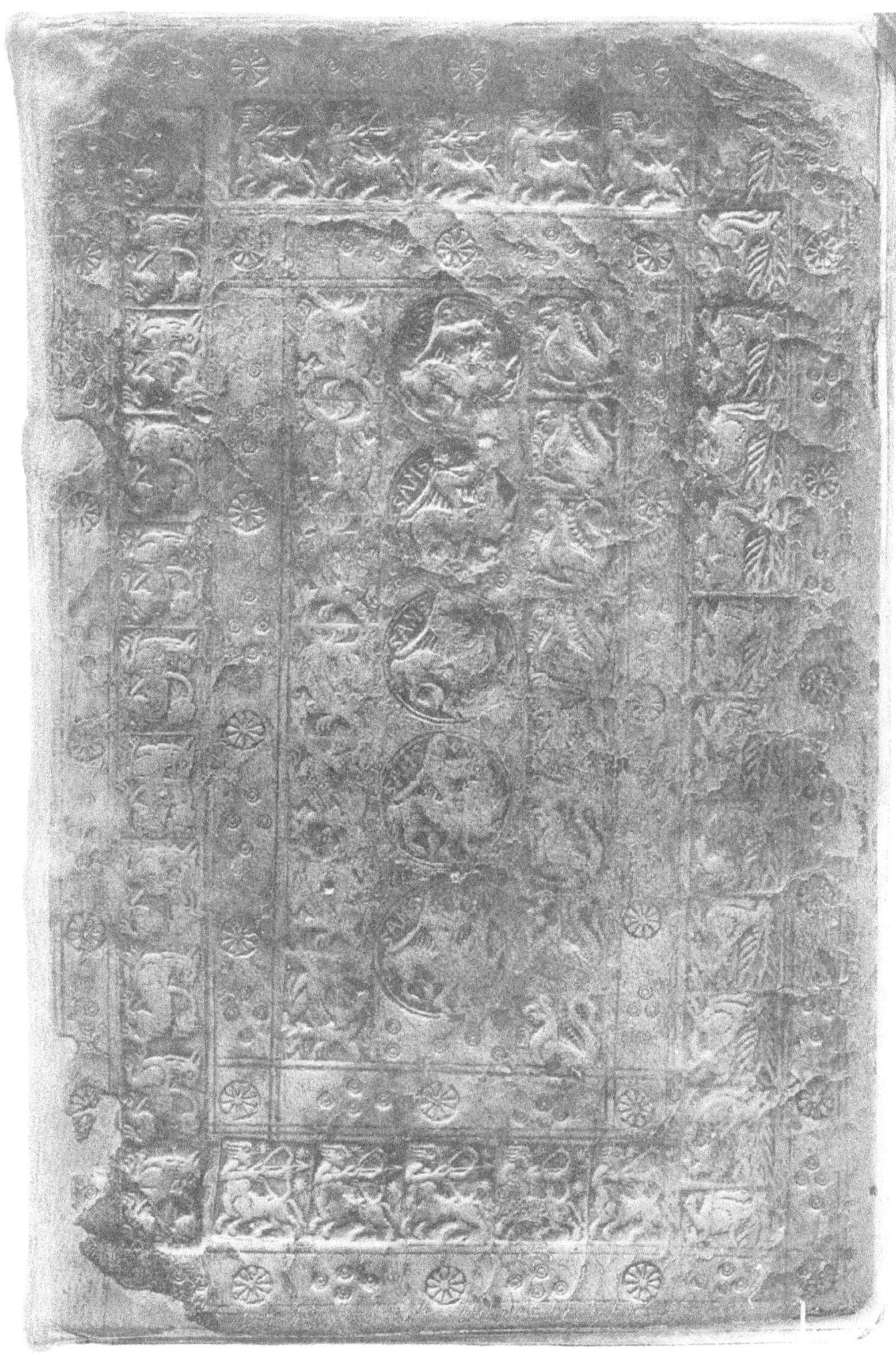

PLATE 29. A Romanesque binding: class P (nationality doubtful). BRITISH MUSEUM, LONDON
List p. 30, No. XIX. *Upper cover.*

PLATE 30. Lower cover of the binding shown on Pl. 29.

PLATE 31. A 13th or 14th-century English binding. See Appendix C, pp. 34–5. *Lower cover.*

CATHEDRAL LIBRARY, DURHAM

PLATE 32 *a*. A 15th-century binding from Jervaulx Abbey. See Appendix J, p. 53, No. 1.
CATHEDRAL LIBRARY, LINCOLN.

PLATE 32 *b*. A ? 14-century French binding. See p. 15.
OWNER UNKNOWN: FROM A MANUSCRIPT SOLD AT SOTHEBY'S

PLATE 33. A Canterbury binding, *c.* 1460. List p. 15, n. 6, No. II. The inscriptions read 'Time Deum'. BODLEY'S LIBRARY, OXFORD

PLATE 34. A Salisbury binding, *c.* 1460. See p. 16. MERTON COLLEGE, OXFORD

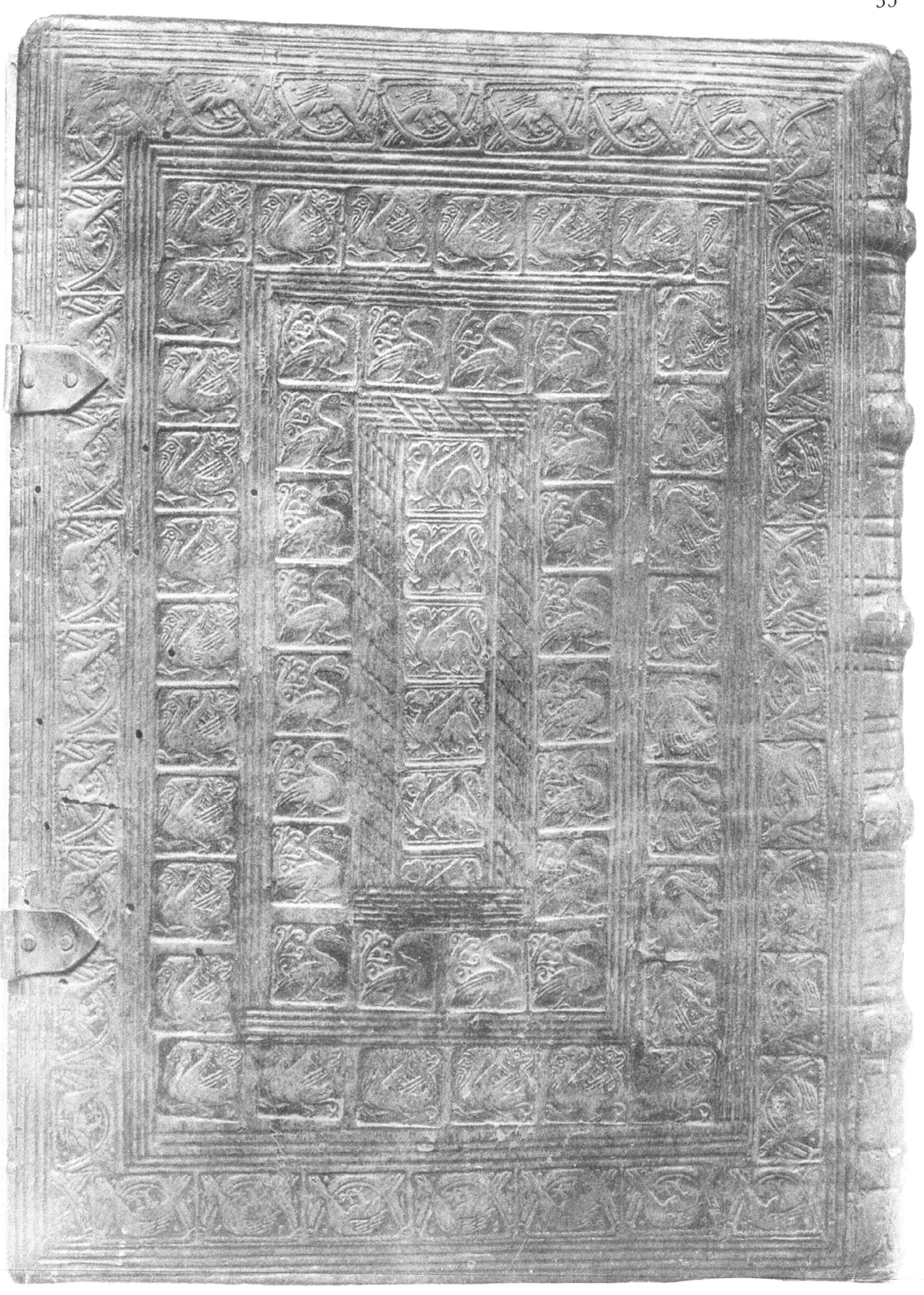

PLATE 35. An Oxford binding, *c.* 1460. See pp. 16–17. See Appendix G, p. 48, No. VIII. BRITISH MUSEUM, LONDON

PLATE 36. An Oxford binding, *c.* 1485. See p. 17.
See Appendix G, p. 48, No. XIX.

UNIVERSITY LIBRARY, CAMBRIDGE

PLATE 37. An Oxford binding, *c.* 1485, by Rood and Hunte's binder. See p. 17. Book printed at Paris 1480. See Weale and Taylor, No. 221.

BRITISH MUSEUM, LONDON. Pressmark I A 39118

PLATE 38. A ? London binding, ? *c.* 1470. See Appendix J, p. 53, No. 11. PEMBROKE COLLEGE, CAMBRIDGE

PLATE 39. A London binding by the 'Scales binder', *c.* 1470: on a late 15th-century English manuscript. See pp. 17–18. Reference: M.R.J. 1186.

TRINITY COLLEGE, CAMBRIDGE

PLATE 40. London 15th-century leatherwork. See p. 18. BRITISH MUSEUM, LONDON

PLATE 41. An English 15th-century leather box. See p. 18.
See Appendix H, p. 50, No. 6.

MOULTON CHURCH, NORFOLK

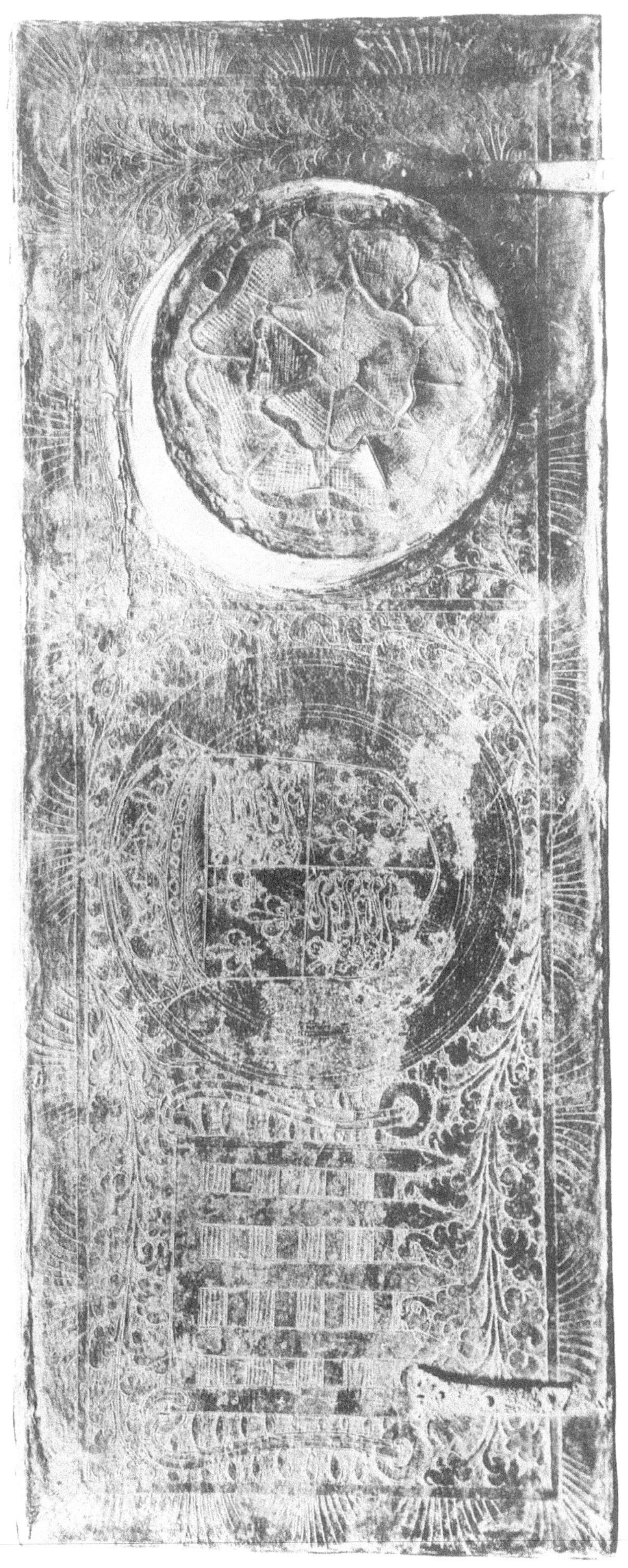

PLATE 41 *a*. A London leather box, 1504. See Appendix H, p. 50, Nos. 10 and 11. PUBLIC RECORD OFFICE, LONDON

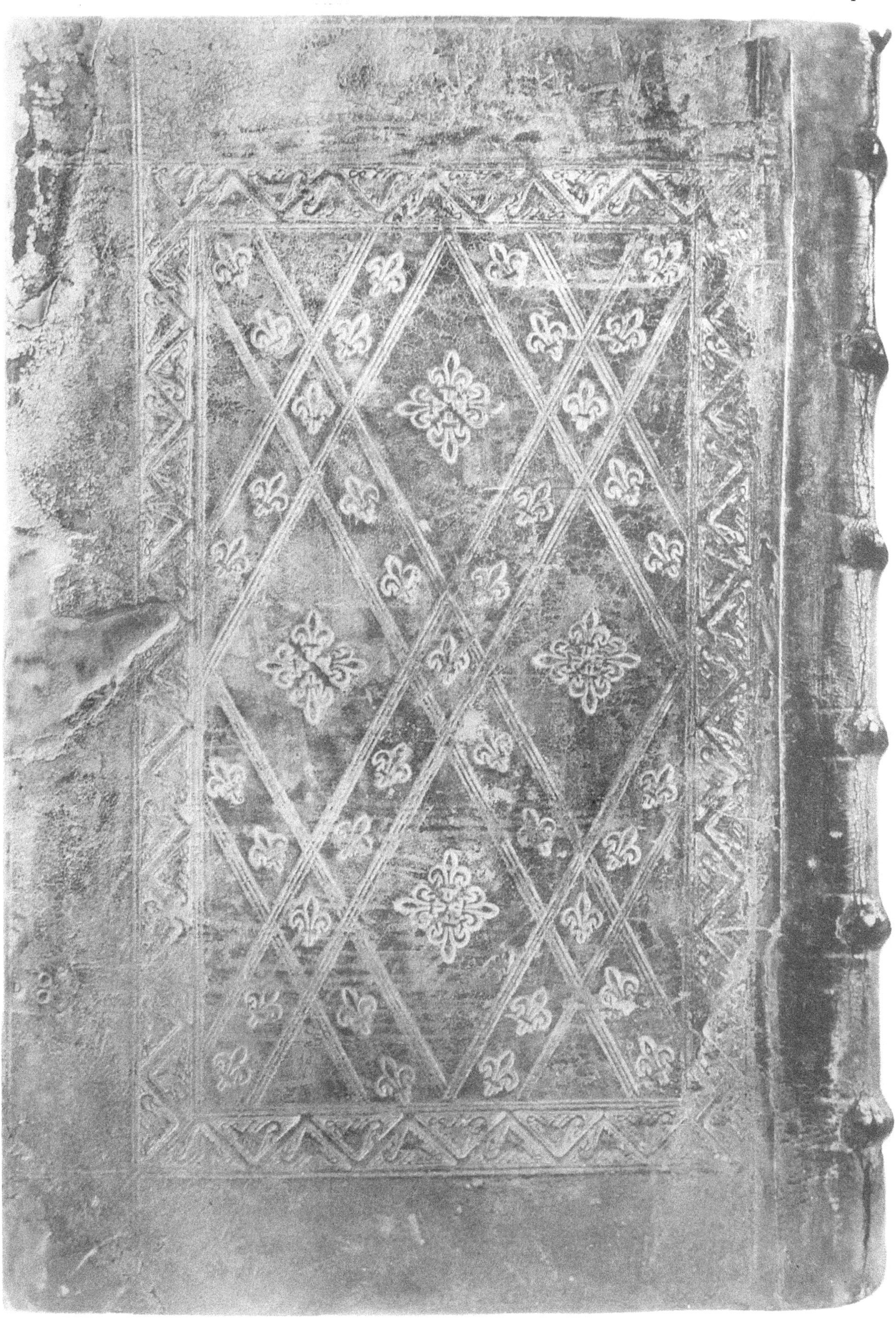

PLATE 42. A binding by Caxton's first binder, *c.* 1485. See p. 19.
Book printed at Oxford, 1483.

CORPUS CHRISTI COLLEGE, CAMBRIDGE
Inc. 113.

PLATE 43. A binding by Caxton's second binder, *c.* 1490. See p. 19. BRITISH MUSEUM, LONDON
Book printed at Westminster, *c.* 1489.

PLATE 44. A late binding by Caxton's second binder, *c.* 1500. See p. 19.

CATHEDRAL LIBRARY, LINCOLN
Inc. 93

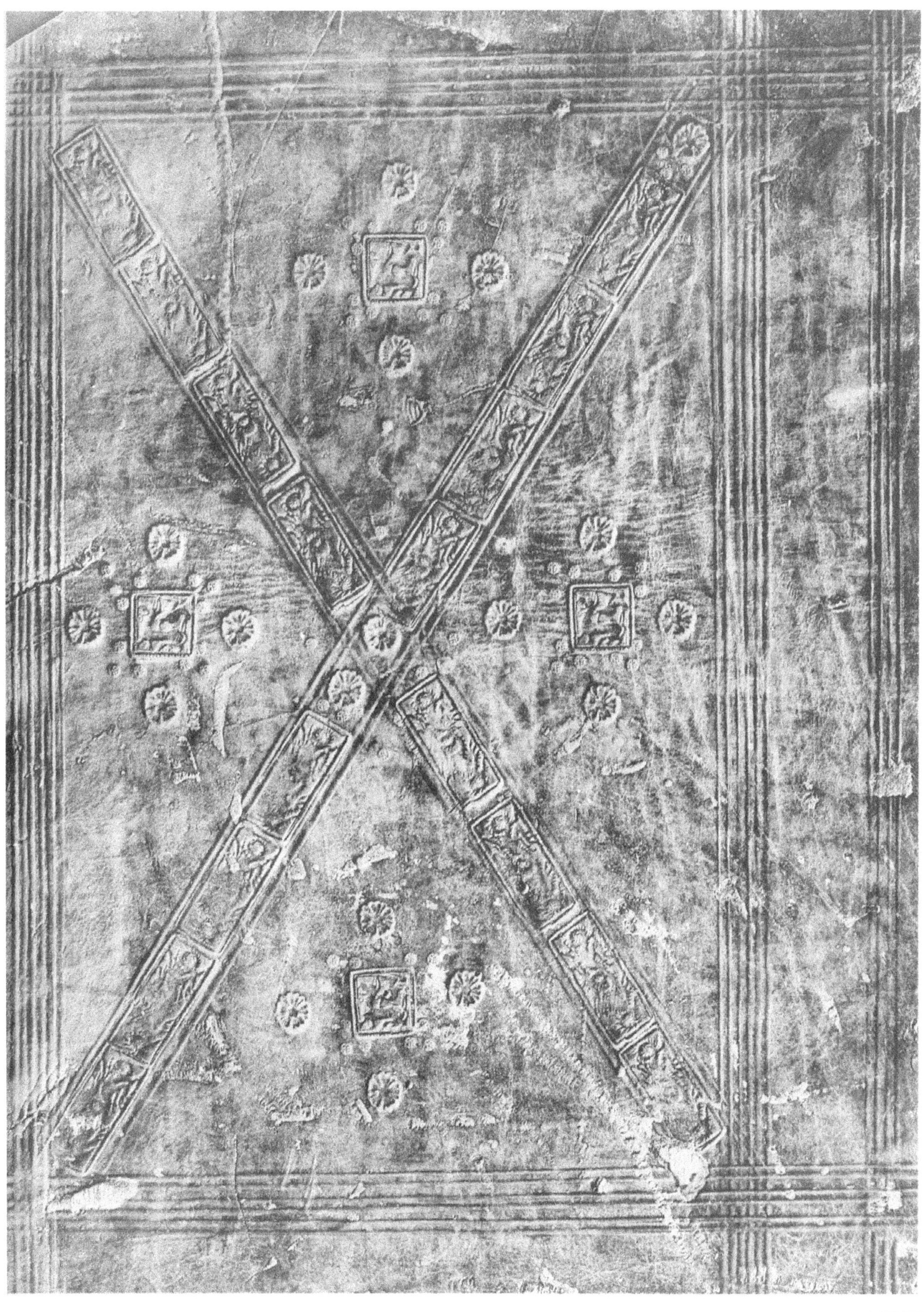

PLATE 45. A London binding by the 'Indulgence binder', *c.* 1480. See p. 20. Book printed at Milan, 1479.

CATHEDRAL LIBRARY, LINCOLN
Inc. 49

PLATE 46. A Cambridge binding by the 'Demon binder', *c.* 1490. See p. 21. Book printed at Nuremberg, *c.* 1489.

PETERHOUSE, CAMBRIDGE
Pressmark O. 2. 5.

PLATE 47. A Cambridge binding by the 'Unicorn binder', *c.* 1485–8. See p. 22. Book printed at Paris, 1480.

JESUS COLLEGE, CAMBRIDGE
Pressmark O. 10. 9.

PLATE 48. A Cambridge binding by the 'Unicorn binder', *c.* 1490–1500. See p. 22.
Various tracts, the latest printed at Vienne, 1490.

BRITISH MUSEUM, LONDON
Pressmark Add. MS. 28,783.

PLATE 49. A Cambridge binding by the 'Unicorn binder', *c.* 1500–5. See p. 22. Book printed at Venice, 1497.

CATHEDRAL LIBRARY, LINCOLN
Inc. 42

PLATE 50. An English or Netherlands binding, *c.* 1490. See Appendix J, p. 54, No. III. Book printed at Brescia, 1482.

CATHEDRAL LIBRARY, LINCOLN
Inc. 51

PLATE 51. A binding with the stamp and roll of W. G. or G. W., *c.* 1510. See pp. 22–3. Book printed at Venice, 1499.

NEW COLLEGE, OXFORD
Pressmark: Auct Wagon 9–16

PLATE 52. A binding by the 'Dragon binder', *c.* 1500. See p. 24, n. 1, No. v. Book printed at Venice, 1497.

CATHEDRAL LIBRARY, LINCOLN
Inc. 44

PLATE 53. A binding by the 'Greyhound binder', 1496–7. See p. 24.
Book printed at Venice, 1496.

CATHEDRAL LIBRARY, WORCESTER

PLATE 54. An English binding, *c.* 1502. See p. 24. Book printed at Venice, 1495.

ABBEY LIBRARY, WESTMINSTER

PLATE 55. An English binding, *c.* 1520. See p. 25. ABBEY LIBRARY, WESTMINSTER
An empty binding.

For EU product safety concerns, contact us at Calle de José Abascal, 56–1°, 28003 Madrid, Spain or eugpsr@cambridge.org.

www.ingramcontent.com/pod-product-compliance
Ingram Content Group UK Ltd.
Pitfield, Milton Keynes, MK11 3LW, UK
UKHW050042190425
457623UK00022B/359
* 9 7 8 0 5 2 1 1 3 7 2 8 7 *